Archive That, Comrade!

KAIROS

In ancient Greek philosophy, *kairos* signifies the right time or the "moment of transition." We believe that we live in such a transitional period. The most important task of social science in time of transformation is to transform itself into a force of liberation. Kairos, an editorial imprint of the Anthropology and Social Change department housed in the California Institute of Integral Studies, publishes groundbreaking works in critical social sciences, including anthropology, sociology, geography, theory of education, political ecology, political theory, and history.

Series editor: Andrej Grubačić

Kairos books:

Practical Utopia: Strategies for a Desirable Society by Michael Albert

In, Against, and Beyond Capitalism: The San Francisco Lectures by John Holloway

Anthropocene or Capitalocene? Nature, History, and the Crisis of Capitalism edited by Jason W. Moore

Birth Work as Care Work: Stories from Activist Birth Communities by Alana Apfel

We Are the Crisis of Capital: A John Holloway Reader by John Holloway

Archive That, Comrade! Left Legacies and the Counter Culture of Remembrance by Phil Cohen

Beyond Crisis: After the Collapse of Institutional Hope in Greece, What? Edited by John Holloway, Katerina Nasioka and Panagiotis Doulos

Re-enchanting the World: Feminism and the Politics of the Commons by Silvia Federici

Occult Features of Anarchism: With Attention to the Conspiracy of Kings and the Conspiracy of the Peoples by Erica Lagalisse

Autonomy Is in Our Hearts: Zapatista Autonomous Government through the Lens of the Tsotsil Language by Dylan Eldredge Fitzwater

Archive That, Comrade!

Left Legacies and the Counter Culture of Remembrance

Phil Cohen

KAIROS

a retort book

a retort book

The Retort imprint publishes books and
pamphlets in the spirit of resistance to capital
and empire, emerging from the collaborative
activity of the Retort group of antinomian
writers, artists, and artisans.

Archive That, Comrade! Left Legacies and the Counter Culture of Remembrance
Phil Cohen
© 2018 PM Press.

ISBN: 978-1-62963-506-4
Library of Congress Control Number: 2017964733

Cover by John Yates / www.stealworks.com
Interior design by briandesign

10 9 8 7 6 5 4 3 2 1

PM Press
PO Box 23912
Oakland, CA 94623
www.pmpress.org

Printed in the USA by the Employee Owners of Thomson-Shore in Dexter, Michigan.
www.thomsonshore.com

In memory of Ste,
beloved adopted son
whose untimely death
created a void
no archive can fill

Contents

LIST OF ILLUSTRATIONS   ix

ACKNOWLEDGEMENTS   xi

PREFACE   xiii

Moot Points   1

Archive Fever: Coming in from the Cold?   4

Counter Culture: Then and Now   10

Ten Days That Shook My World: Remembering 144 Piccadilly
between Spectacle and Trauma   13

In My End Is Others' Beginning: Left Legacy Politics
and the Dialectic of Generations   22

Winners and Losers   31

Let Us Now Praise Famous People: Paradigms of Remembrance
and the Twin Cultures of Modernity   37

Fame Academies   46

On Memes and other Mnemonic Devices   48

Technologies of Immortality   53

Towards a Theory of Archival Genres   56

A Tale of Two Archives   63

Between *Realpolitik* and *Dingpolitik*: The Living Archive
in a 'Post-information' Age   78

The Adoptive Archive: A Thought Experiment   80

Left Field and the Quest for Uncommon Ground   82

Lest We Remember, Lest We Forget: On Iconoclasm and the
Problematics of Silence   85

Archival In/Disciplines   90

Curating the Anarchive   93

Not Everyone Will Be Taken into the Future   97

The Arc of Memory   102

Postscript: The Politics of False Memory in the Age of 'Post-Truth'   104

NOTES   107

FURTHER READING   120

ABOUT THE AUTHOR   128

INDEX   129

List of Illustrations

Dr John photograph   19
Don't Mourn, Organise   26
The Museum of Innocence   42
L'Archiviste (Schuiten and Peeters)   52
Demonstration to remove the statue of Cecil Rhodes from the facade
of Oriel College, Oxford   54
The Black Cultural Archive   64
Infoshop 56a   70, 73
Monument against Fascism, Hamburg   89
Goshka Macuga, *Death of Marxism, Women of All Lands Unite*, 2013   103

Acknowledgements

I would like to thank Iain Boal for convening the original deposition event at the MayDay Rooms, for encouraging me to elaborate on those initial remarks, and for his many editorial comments. I would also like to thank Tim Clark for his detailed and perceptive comments on an early draft and for his very useful suggestions on how to improve it. Neither of the above should be held responsible for any of the views or arguments expressed here. Thanks also to all those friends and comrades who attended the MayDay Rooms event for their contributions to the discussion, which I have drawn on extensively in revising the text of the talk for publication. I owe a special debt of gratitude to Ross Bradshaw of Five Leaves, the publisher of my memoir, *Reading Room Only*, for inviting me to talk at a conference of trade-union and community activists in Nottingham, which first prompted these deliberations. Finally I would like to thank Donald Nicholson-Smith for his encouragement, for his many useful editorial suggestions, and for helping see the project through to publication. As always, my partner Jean McNeil has provided much shrewd counsel and support, bringing a painter's eye to the detail of the argument; she also came to my rescue in helping source the references for the bibliography.

Phil Cohen, Wivenhoe and London, December 2017

Preface

Not so long ago I had the experience of mentoring a young German student who was intensely curious about British culture and society and what had shaped it in the second half of the twentieth century. He plied me with questions such as: 'What was it like before Mrs Thatcher?'; 'How does the situation of gay people today compare with what it was like in the 1960s?'; 'When did Damien Hirst first become famous?'; 'How did people in this country respond to the fall of the Berlin Wall?'; 'Have British people always not liked immigrants?' I did not always find it easy to answer him without falling into what Marx called 'dumb generalities', but I did my best to point him in the direction of where the answers might be found. Quite often I ended up telling him stories about my own political involvements when I was his age, in the 1960s. After one such episode, he turned to me and said, 'Dude, you know, you're a real archivist!' I did not know whether to be flattered or to read this as a wind-up *cum* put-down to the effect that my experience no longer had any relevance to the present and was simply of historical interest, but it became apparent that he meant it as a genuine compliment. After all, he came from a society which had tried to get a whole postwar generation to forget about its immediate past, and where opening up the archives revealed all kinds of previously hidden and painful facts.

It is, of course, very gratifying to be asked about one's past by someone much younger who is as interested in its political dimensions as its personal ones. Even the so-called selfie generation occasionally come out of their reverie, look about and fasten on some figure that can tell once-upon-a-lifetime stories about what the world was like before they were born.

xiii

Still, I had never considered myself to be an archivist. I had a small collection of magazines, posters and other ephemera from the period (1965–78) when I was active in the London underground scene, but it never occurred to me that anyone would call it an archive or be interested in what it contained. But then, I reflected, nowadays everyone is an archivist of some sort. An archival reflex is programmed into every form of research and knowledge production, and through our digital devices we have an instant archiving system to hand. Moreover, in reaction to living in a throwaway society people collect all manner of things. There is no object too trivial or ephemeral to be invested with special meaning as a collectible worthy to be catalogued: beer mats, bottle tops, stickers. Scavenging for scraps of memory in the detritus of consumerism is the stuff many do-it-yourself archives are now made of.

So, as the reader will become all too aware, I am not a professional archivist or a trained historian. In fact I studied history in my first year at University, but even then the dim awareness that archival research was an essential rite of passage for the professional historian was enough to put me off.[1] I switched to anthropology, where fieldwork had the same ritual function but promised exciting present-tense encounters with real, living others rather than having to burrow like Hegel's old mole through mounds of dusty documents, attempting to resurrect the dead and throw up new insights into the darker, more hidden aspects of their worlds. Yet anthropology, as I was soon to discover, has its own archival anxieties bound up with its colonial past.[2] As an ethnographer I became interested in what people remember and forget, what they hold on to or jettison as they struggle to make sense of their lives unfolding in particular times and places, in other words in the whole process of do-it-yourself archiving. Most of my working life has been spent with communities experiencing extreme dislocation as the economic, social and cultural landscape shifts under their feet. In these circumstances, the archive as a metaphor or model of what can be said in the future about the present, when it will have become the past, takes on great salience, even and especially for those groups who have no direct access to the official apparatus of the public record but nevertheless find their existence overrepresented there, usually in the most reductive statistical terms.

When I was invited to contribute some material to an archive of the 1960s counter culture set up recently by the MayDay Rooms, it prompted me to think in more general terms about the place of the archive in contemporary memory politics. This essay explores some of the wider issues of archival theory and practice which arise with special acuteness for projects which have a Left political agenda and which also aspire to provide an open-access platform for dialogue and democratic debate. These reflections are also informed by the experience of writing a memoir that included an account of the occupation of 144 Piccadilly, an event which hit the world's headlines for ten days in July 1969 but has since been largely ignored by historians of the counter culture. This prompted me to consider the political and cultural legacy of the 'alternative society' in relation to the '60s spectacle of 'youth revolt' and the social amnesia disseminated by our culture of instant, do-it-yourself celebrity. In a way that I had not anticipated when I started writing, this focus took on topical, if possibly transient, relevance as the fiftieth anniversary of May '68 arrived and with it a flurry of events designed to either celebrate or critically evaluate the legacy of that particular 'youthquake'. This coincidence in turn has made me think about the transmission of political ideas and cultural values across the generations, and how this has been affected by the emergence of new technologies of remembrance.

My discussion begins by setting the scene with a commentary on a series of quotes which illustrate some of the key issues in contemporary debates around the archive. This is followed by a diary of what immediately occasioned its writing, with a consideration of the legacy of the 1960s counter culture. Does the 'alternative society' require an alternative kind of archive to adequately represent its ethos? As a test case I introduce some material from my personal collection and discuss what happens to these personal mementos when they are translated into a public medium through the act of archival consignment.

The argument then broadens out to consider the memory politics of the Left, and how these are shaped by its models of historical explanation, its principles of hope, and the generational transmission of its values and ideals. How far is it possible to sustain a counter culture of commemoration, centred on collective memory in the face of the ever-expanding apparatus of individual celebrity and fame relayed through both corporate and social media? How, in more general terms, is posthumous identity sustained in the age of Instagram and Facebook?

The essay goes on to examine the limits and conditions of archival reason in, and sometimes against, digital culture; it develops a typology of archival genres, drawing on recent debates in narratology and memory studies, and this model is applied to an ethnographic reading of two radical archives with very different political agendas and modes of organisation.

The sheer volume and variety of archival projects on the culture of the Left gives the lie to those who argue that it is in the terminal stages of decline, although, as I discuss in the main text, there is always a risk that archive building may draw energies away from political activism, or become a substitute for it.

The final sections of the text explore different aspects of the Living Left 'Anarchive', looking in some detail at issues of internal organisation, agenda setting, public access and dissemination, which arise whenever a sustained attempt is made to create a platform not just for the conservation of political memoryscapes but to encourage open debate over their legacy as a portal into the imagination of a better future. A postscript examines the rise of the alt-right and its annexing of the populist archive to create a regime of false political memory.

As this is an essay, it eschews the polemical or didactic drive of the political pamphlet, consisting rather of a number of lines of thought taken for a walk around its key themes. Nor is it an academic treatise, although some of the intellectual hinterland is outlined in footnotes and in a guide to further reading.

I am all too aware that this text draws on a culturally limited range of examples and that the argument applies primarily to the archival politics of advanced Western capitalist societies. The impact of mnemonic technologies plays out very differently on the Indian subcontinent, in China and in Islamic countries; it would require another essay to do justice to these complexities, even if I were qualified to address them. Nearer to home in terms of cultural geography, I think that readers in the Americas, mainland Europe and Australasia will not have too much difficulty in recognising the trends I am discussing and will easily be able to identify local parallels, even though most of my examples are drawn from the British context.

My primary purpose in writing this has been to worry at a number of questions about the role of the archive which have preoccupied scholar activists in recent years, be they oral historians, cultural geographers, ethnographers, narratologists or visual artists, each in their own way engaged in research involving marginalised groups on the front line of social and economic change. More broadly I have tried to address some of the public concerns about the advent of digital culture. In particular I look at its impact on the use of the archive as a democratic platform for shifting the terms of debate around social injustice beyond the frame imposed by the neoliberal agenda. I hope at least to persuade readers who, like my younger self, thought that archives were dim and dusty places only frequented by academic zombies in search of obscure historical references or demented bureaucrats following audit trails, that they constitute an increasingly important site of struggle over not just the past but the future.

Notes

1　See Carolyn Steedman, *Dust: The Archive and Cultural History* (2016) for an impassioned defence of the traditional archive as well as a critique of Derrida's speculative deconstruction of it.
2　See Ann Laura Stoler, *Along the Archival Grain: Epistemic Anxieties and Colonial Common Sense* (2009).

Moot Points

archive: 1. From Greek *arkheia*, things kept at the public office, derived from *arche*, beginning, government; 2. A collection of documents such as letters, official papers, photographs or recorded material kept for their historical interest; 3. Backup computer file, kept often in compressed form on tape or disk for long-term storage; a directory of files that Internet users can access using File Transfer Protocol. —*Encarta World English Dictionary*

Ark: something that affords protection and safety; a chest or cupboard holding the scrolls of the Torah in a synagogue; a low hut used to house livestock; a ship or boat. —*Oxford English Dictionary*

An archive is where Mr and Mrs Noah and all the animals went to get out of the rain, but it rained and rained for 40 days and nights, so they just stayed put, luckily they had taken lots of story and picture books along with them so they weren't bored. —*primary school pupil*

It takes time for what has been erased to surface. Traces survive in registers, and nobody knows where these registers are hidden, and who has custody of them, and whether or not their custodians are willing to let you see them. Or perhaps they have forgotten that such registers exist. —Patrick Modiano, *Search Warrant*

Just as voluntary memory and utter oblivion belong together, so organised fame and remembrance lead ineluctably to nothingness. —Theodor Adorno, *Minima Moralia*

Modern memory is above all archival. It relies entirely on the materialities of the trace, the immediacy of records, the visibility of the image. What began as writing ends in high fidelity and tape recording. No longer living memories, more or less intended remainders, the archive has become the deliberate and calculated secretion of lost memory. It adds to life, itself often a function of its own recording, a secondary memory, a prosthesis-memory. —Pierre Nora, *Les Lieux de mémoire*

The starting point of critical elaboration is the question of what one really is, 'knowing thyself' as a product of historical processes to date which have deposited in you an infinity of traces, without leaving an inventory—therefore it is imperative at the outset to compile such an inventory. —Antonio Gramsci, *The Prison Notebooks*

The function of the archive, as of art, is to hold unlikely things. . . . The primary operations of the archive are no longer the contents of its files but rather their logistical interlinking, just as the Web is not primarily defined by its contents but by its protocols. —Wolfgang Ernst, *Digital Memory and the Archive*

The question of the archive is not a question of the past. . . . It is a question of the future, the question of the future itself, the question of a response, of a promise, and of a responsibility for tomorrow. . . . Effective democratization can always be measured by this essential criterion: the participation in and the access to the archive. —Jacques Derrida, *Archive Fever*

We should not be deceived into thinking that heritage is an acquisition, a possession that grows and solidifies; rather it is an unstable assemblage of faults, fissures, and heterogeneous layers that threaten the fragile inheritor from within or from underneath. —Michel Foucault, 'Nietzsche, Genealogy, History'

The old word 'thing' or 'ding' originally meant a certain type of assembly. The point of reviving this old notion of assembly in a contemporary notion of assemblage, is that we don't assemble because we agree, look alike, feel good, are socially compatible, but because we are brought together by divisive matters of concern into some neutral isolated place in order to arrive at some sort of provisional makeshift (dis)agreement. —Bruno Latour, 'From Realpolitik to Dingpolitik or How to Make Things Public'

Moot
Noun: 1) An assembly held for debate in Anglo-Saxon and mediaeval times
2) A mock proceeding set up to examine a hypothetical case as an academic exercise
Verb: To raise or broach a question or topic for discussion
Adjective: 1) Subject to debate, dispute, uncertainty
2) Having little or no practical relevance

Fever: Coming in from the Cold?

...d's confusion of the Ark with the archive in the preceding quote makes us smile, as if it were no more than a charming elision of sounds and meaning, but the association of the two words points to a significant but often overlooked point of connection between them. The archive is a safe harbour for all manner of materials, artefacts, texts, images, documents, which might otherwise perish, whether from neglect or active suppression. It is an affordance of memory which may be a container of profane narratives or holy scripts, bureaucratic protocols or autobiographical memories, but it restores their capacity to survive the storms of history which produced them. The archive is an ark of the covenant we all make with the world in which we struggle to make our mark on posterity. What might appear initially to be a mere container of accidental traces of the past turns out, on closer inspection, to be an object of calculation, even intervention, albeit one that is largely disavowed.

Yet this arch-mnemonic can also be a trap, a siren call to unwary historians, a seductive invitation to immerse themselves in an oceanic feeling of omniscience about the past or, conversely, to drown in sea of nostalgic identification with lives other than their own. The archive can be a talisman for the multifarious desire to 'get to the bottom of things' which may start off with innocent acts of curiosity but all too often ends by being driven by an obsessive ambition to capture and sum up the world. Patrick Modiano draws our attention to an even less attractive face of the archive, its capacity to conceal, to resist disclosure, to obfuscate, even to cover its own tracks so that its existence is either unknown or mere rumour. So it is not only a question of what is lost by being excluded from the archive, but also what remains buried or hidden within it.

A good case in point are the British colonial archives held at Hanslope Park, whose existence was denied for many years because they contain information which gives the lie to the official 'legacy archives' bequeathed by colonial administrations to the newly independent states of the Commonwealth. These provided a highly selective record of events designed to leave behind a positive image of Britain's colonial legacy and eliminate all traces of an often brutal and oppressive regime from the collective memory, a residuum of historical fact which is all too much in evidence at Hanslope Park. The tension between Public Record Acts and the Official Secrets Act remains a constant in the UK story of the archive's troubled relation to the nation-state.[1]

4

Archives can also serve as a platform for the guardianship of unofficial secrets in civil society. For example, there is the Ark of the Apostles Society, a secret society of a budding intellectual elite at Cambridge between the wars which at one time included many of the Bloomsbury Group. The ark is a wooden box, now housed in Kings College Archive Centre, which contains a diary of the society's proceedings and copies of the papers its members gave. Although the existence of the society was for a long time an open secret, its membership, and hence access to the Ark, remained closed and confined to a coterie of the initiated who were all undergraduate or graduate students of Kings College and St John's.[2]

Yet the self-conscious concealment of knowledge by an intellectual elite is something of a special case. The demand to 'open the archive', whether on the lips of those whose loved ones have been disappeared by State violence, adoptees trying to discover who their birth parents are, or historians trying to gain access to official documents, this demand has largely been addressed to the state and its bureaucracy. The notion of an open archive, which the demand implies, has ramifications for a democratised memory politics which we will explore.[3]

The dual nature of the conventional archive, poised as it is between the inert storing of classified information and its active appropriation, is widely recognised. For Pierre Nora this reiterates the classic Platonic distinction between two different forms of memory, one based oral communication and the other on the written record and prosthetic technology. It has also been argued that the archive occupies a special liminal space between these two positions, in which documents—and the lives or events whose traces they bear—exist in a kind of limbo, neither in the world of the living nor the dead but awaiting their moment of resurrection in the hands of an archivist who will bring them into the light of day.[4]

From this starting point, there are divergent perspectives on the potential of the archive to challenge the dominant forms of knowledge/power in which it has been historically embedded. Foucault, Derrida and Latour all converge on a single idea—that the role of the archive is to provide a public space of deliberation and debate in which traditions can be unsettled, ideologies contested, familiar history defamiliarised. The archive is a way of bringing unlikely things together in order to take their established associations apart and in doing so it stakes out uncommon ground. You may think that this is a moot point, especially if you consider the word's etymology. The Witenagemot was a powerful group of 'wise men', a.k.a. nobles and churchmen, who assembled to counsel the king, but in certain areas where the royal writ did not run, the moot could take on a more popular democratic form, albeit one that has been somewhat over-egged by those on the left who want to see it as an early or 'primitive' form of communist society.[5] The verb certainly suggests that the purpose of such assembly should be to exercise the dialogic imagination and practice the arts of disputation. Even more suggestive for our purposes is the notion of an archive as a site where information may be assembled in order to conduct thought experiments, to test out different explanations against the evidence. But then, of course, there is always the risk that this will degenerate into a purely academic exercise, of little practical relevance.

In what follows I shall be mooting a number of possible approaches to understanding the democratic potential of the archive. My central question is this: does it actually require that the archive occupy an isolated neutral space, as Latour suggests, for this purpose? Or can it also be an intervention which sets up new and critically engaged forms of dialogue, both within and beyond the material itself?

Secondly, does the process of archival reframing not also require an opposite movement to which it is dialectically related—a moment of conservation, or consolidation, a process of re-concentration of what has been disassembled and dispersed? Seen from an anthropological perspective the archival impulse can be regarded as a form of ritual defence against the furies potentially released by the fragmentation of a legacy, a way of pacifying the spirits of the dead, in providing some principle of interpretive closure to protect the living from endless disputes over ancestral virtues or vices they may (or may not) inherit. But how does this tension between the compulsion to repeat the past and the desire to escape it play out in actual strategies of collection and curation and what kind of memory politics do these strategies imply?

The quotation from Adorno draws our attention to the negative dialectic which might exist between the archival drive as a denial of transience, mortality, and death and the apparatus of celebrity which ephemeralises life to the point where the posterity of fame is nullified.

In contrast, Gramsci suggests that an inventory of traces, whether invoking the genealogy of subjects or objects, is a necessary condition for understanding their real—which is to say historical—conditions of existence. In this context, Benjamin's Arcades Project, which consisted of a series of folders—or 'convolutes'—containing diverse material on particular aspects of nineteenth-century Paris, not only gives unique surreal expression to the archival form but can also be considered a Gramscian inventory of traces. The project also laid the foundations for elaborating a theory of the capitalist city as a cultural assemblage, a site of chaotic synchronicity, which his collagist technique was designed to capture.[6]

The impulse to make inventories can move in opposite directions, however. For Gramsci's organic working-class intellectual it involves becoming free enough of ideological conditioning to be able to act back on the world in a self-conscious and reflexive way. For Benjamin's bourgeois collector it means stripping the object of everything worldly (including the labour that produced it) that would prevent it becoming a prop in the psychodrama of the collector's secret passion. So here again we have the two faces of the archive, one turned outwards to the public domain and the manifold sites of its transformation, the other turned inwards to assemble, with obsessive precision, a private model of its detailed workings in a specific sphere of human endeavour. Yet however prescient their methodology, neither Gramsci nor Benjamin could have anticipated a digital culture in which historical time and autobiographical time diverge so radically, giving rise to an 'archive fever' designed to stitch them back together again into a simulated coherence through a wild variety of mash-ups.

Wolfgang Escher draws a vivid distinction between the traditional archive, in which cultural memory is still anchored to the archive's capacity to store and classify material information (artefacts, documents) within an interpretive or meta-narrative frame, and the virtual or digital archive where algorithms have become a kind of automated mnemonic device, with an infinite capacity for enlargement and updating. For evangelists of the virtual archive, like Ernst, the open-access platform is an instrument for the democratisation of knowledge power; in contrast those, like Arlette Farge, who remain committed to a hands-on model of archival research, the primary encounter with the material is multi-sensorial and cannot be reduced to the mere scanning of images or texts. But can the very materiality of the document, far from being a guarantee of the authentic facticity of what it records, not be deceptive, even a statement of fake news?

My interest in this question goes back to a visit to a museum in East Berlin in 1980. The museum portended to tell the story of the creation of the GDR as a bulwark of socialism in the front line of the cold war. As you entered the large portico you were confronted with a steam locomotive, resplendent in the colours of the GDR. Children were enjoying climbing into the cab and imagining themselves driving it down the tracks. But where did these imaginary tracks lead? If you looked closely at the base of the engine you could read a small plaque announcing that this was one of trains which had hauled bricks to help build the Berlin Wall, constructed entirely with volunteer labour, by workers who were defending socialism against its enemies. A story then of East Berliners enthusiastically volunteering to cut themselves off from their families and friends in the West, and to live in an open prison from which many of them died trying to escape. So here we had an artefact transformed into a protagonist in a narrative which its presence authorises and which is in fact a piece of state propaganda. The very materiality of the exhibit provides its alibi as a mute witness to the fabrication of a historical untruth. Another way to put this is to say that the archival object is falsified by what it is made to verify within the archival frame.

About ten years later I revisited Berlin in very different circumstances. The Wall had fallen and the Museum of Hysterical Materialism, as I nicknamed it, was closed.[7] I had been invited to speak at a conference about racism organised by the reconstituted Socialist Unity Party which had ruled the old GDR and was now trying to reinvent itself as a social democratic party carrying the banner for the 'Ossies' who were finding themselves second-class citizens in the new united Germany. The conference was attended mainly by party delegates, sad-looking middle-aged men wearing grey or brown raincoats who had been part of the old *nomenklatura* but now found themselves unemployed. One of them, let me call him Max, who took me under his wing and whom I got to know quite well, had been a member of the Stasi. He confessed that the worst thing about what had happened was not that he had become a social pariah and an object of general opprobrium but that he had been forced to recognise that his whole life had been wasted in pursuit of a dream that turned out to be a nightmare. The opening of the Stasi archives had revealed just how deeply embedded the state surveillance system had been and the large numbers of citizens who had collaborated with it, whether out of fear or a genuine sense of patriotic duty. Like many of his fellow militants, Max had been a member of the *Kamfgruppen der Arbeiterclasse*, the GDR's ideological shock troops, and like them he had volunteered to help build

8

the Wall. To prove his change of heart he offered me a small fragment of brightly graffitied stone which he assured me he had personally chipped out of the Wall. When I got back to my hotel I compared it with another piece of the Wall embedded in a postcard I had bought, which had been issued to celebrate the events of 1989. It was also graffitied but was of a quite different composition. Perhaps it was from a different part of the Wall, but was it possible that one of these stones was a fake? After the fall of the Wall tens of thousands of people went hunting for souvenirs, and a whole export industry grew up around distributing fragments as holy reliquaries of this historic moment across the world. Once the remains of the Wall were protected, some East Berliners, desperate to cash in, turned themselves into do-it-yourself archivists and began to 'manufacture' this little bit of history in their own backyards.

There are two conclusions to be drawn from this experience which are the starting points for the reflections that follow. The first is that that the knowledge power of the archive, once in the hands of the state, is absolute; even if it is not directly employed as an instrument of propaganda, it can be a means of censorship and occlusion as well as selective remembrance. And it can become an affordance for the most intrusive technologies of control. Today, with the growing datafication of every aspect of our interaction with the state and the market, as citizens and consumers we find that we are unwitting and often unwilling accomplices in a vast operation to extract, monitor, commodify and archive information about the most intimate aspects of our everyday lives. Our computers and mobile devices leak geo-located data about our life style patterns, sexual preferences, social networks and journeys around town, creating an involuntary memoryscape to which we are denied access. If the Benthamite panopticon was the model of surveillance and regulation in early capitalist society, the virtual archive is the model of the control society of late modernity.[8]

The second point stands against the first; it is that the archival significance of objects cannot be secured by their mode of production or material provenance alone. Under hypnosis a bricklayer can remember and distinguish between every single brick he has laid in the previous week, according to its texture and other features. Even mass-produced objects have a singularity of use not reducible to their social typification so that any attempt to enclose their meaning within a totalising frame of reference is doomed to failure. There is no doubt which of my pieces of the Berlin Wall tells the more interesting story; even if Max's gift turned out be fake, the narrative it served to prompt verifies its authenticity for the same reason that makes its provenance unreliable. This uncoupling of provenance and meaning *is* the challenge of archival interpretation. As he said to me, with a slight twinkle in his eye, as he finished the story and pressed the precious stone into my hand, 'Archive that, comrade!'

Counter Culture: Then and Now

The immediate prompt for this text was being asked to give a talk to a conference about a memoir I had written, describing, among other things, my involvements in 1960s counter culture.[9] The conference brought together local trade union and community activists to debate the question: is there still a working class? This put me in something of a quandary: what on earth could a piece of writing that was mainly about growing up in a middle-class family in Bloomsbury during and after the Second World War, about the experience of being educated in an elite school, then dropping out of Cambridge and running away to join the counter culture of the Sixties, and most of all about collecting, stealing, reading and writing books—what on earth could such a text have to say to a meeting of mainly working-class activists, most of whom had not even been born in 1969?

The talk had been billed as revisiting the 'Revolutionary Sixties'. Along with a few choice quotes from the text, the blurb raised expectations of a trip down memory lane, with perhaps a little gentle debunking of the myth of the 'youth revolution' en route, plus a graphic account of my night of passion with Allen Ginsberg. The old saw that 'if you can remember the Sixties, you weren't there' may be a good in-joke about collateral brain damage caused by taking too much LSD, but there certainly has been no shortage of memoirs of the period by its survivors. Many of these accounts regale drug-fuelled exploits with a rueful panache that draws on the long-established theme of sowing wild oats, while others gesture towards a never-coming-of-age story predicated on the proposition that 'it is never too late to have a happy childhood'.

In my case the memoir traced my coming-of-age story from school rebel and apprentice bohemian to counter cultural provocateur, and thence to street activist and lefty academic. Yet even in such a familiar trajectory it is not always easy to detect the undertow of influences. A few years ago I was a member of a reminiscence group of 1960s radicals, drawn from both Europe and the Americas, in which we tried, by comparing our life stories, to detect some common patterns or strands in our various engagements which ranged from armed struggle to cultural avant-gardism and from feminism to internationalism. Perhaps unsurprisingly the differences in our experiences were easier to articulate than our commonalities.

Yet even as I tried to concentrate my talk on linking personal and political history, I still had to ask myself why should anybody who is politically active today bother about what happened, or didn't happen all those years ago? Supposing for a moment that there is more to this particular conjuncture than could be retrieved through reminiscence work with groups of ageing hippies or retired left-wing academics, what possible significance could 'flower power' or the student protests against the Vietnam War have for Generation Rent? What could the children of postwar affluence, the never-had-it-so-good generation of baby boomers, for whom precarity was an ideological stance or transient lifestyle choice, have to say to the children of austerity, the never-had-it-so-bad generation for whom precarity has become a chronic condition of existence?[10]

The short answer has to be that the counter culture, in its many manifestations, might be seen as prefigurative of much of what was to come, and its legacy is still with us, which is one reason why it is so hotly contested. It is still a tacit reference point, both negative and positive, for much contemporary political debate on the left. In one, mainly Marxist, reading it is a cautionary tale.[11] It marks a historical turning point in which the project of political emancipation founded on the industrial working class auto-destructs. The onward march of labour is permanently halted well this side of the New Jerusalem while capitalism goes cultural as well as global, and becomes hip. The so-called 'Youth Revolution' creates a platform for disseminating the hedonistic pleasure principles of consumerism and makes possessive individualism—doing your own thing—sexy, addictive and above all cool. Recreational sex, drugs and rock'n'roll may not exactly be the devil's work, but they promote the dispositions of creative self-invention, underpinned by a whole culture of narcissism that post-Fordism, and the just-in-time production of the self requires. Playing it cool becomes the motto of a whole 'post' generation: postmodernist, post-Marxist, post-feminist, post-political.[12] From this standpoint the 'counter culture' is well named, for it is precisely about the merchandising of pseudo-radical life styles, getting your highs from what you can buy or sell *across the counter* in a way which lends itself to constant recycling and retro-chic.[13]

Another reading, which comes mainly from the libertarian Left, sees 1960s counter culture as a great disseminator of a popular anti-authoritarian politics, a generational revolt against the patriarchal structures of the family and the bureaucratic structures of state and corporate culture, and as such embarked on the quest for new and more directly democratic forms of collective self-organisation, based on a moral economy of mutual aid. It is also about an aesthetic revolt against the dead weight of elite bourgeois literary and artistic canons and cultural tastes. A rejection then of party politics, whether mainstream or vanguardist, in the name of a cultural avant-gardism embedded in everyday life. This version of the counter culture is celebrated as an incubator of new counter-hegemonic visions, associated variously with feminism, gay liberation, antiracism, the environmentalist movement, community activism and do-it-yourself urbanism. It prefigures the antiglobalisation and anticapitalist movements of more recent years as well as radical identity politics.[14]

Every interpretation of the counter culture tends to privilege some aspects over others as symptomatic. Culturalist interpretations emphasise the global impact on music, fashion and other creative industries. Clothes, posters, record covers and other ephemeral artefacts provide a readymade archive for curating such a viewpoint, often drawn from the personal collections of the alternative glitterati.[15] In contrast, political commentators focus on the student and antiwar movements and their often tense and tenuous relationship to traditional Left and labour organisations.[16]

Some of the more elaborate analyses recognise that alternative life styles could have both progressive and reactionary aspects, could challenge the patriarchal biopolitics of deferred gratification *and* be part of what Marcuse called the apparatus of repressive desublimation.[17] However, most of the personal accounts produced about this period emphasise the positive, liberatory aspects, whether they concentrate on the cultural or the political dimension.

Now clearly what we refer to rather glibly as the '60s counter culture is a complicated affair: it is made up of many different strands and is not homogeneous either ideologically or sociologically. For a start, the 'alternative society' in Britain mirrored the stratifications of so-called straight society. It had its aristocracy, some of them the rebellious offspring of actual aristocrats or plutocrats but mostly wealthy rock musicians and entrepreneurs who bankrolled its projects. It had its professional middle class who ran its organisations, like BIT, Release and the underground press.[18] And then it had its foot soldiers, the young people who flocked to its psychedelic colours and lived on the margins.

One of my motives in writing my memoir *Reading Room Only* was to insist that the university and the creative industries were not the only or even the most important sites of ferment. The squatting movement and what was happening on the streets made their own platform of ideas and practices.[19] My hope was that the material I brought along to deposit in the archive would enable the street commune movement and in particular the occupation of 144 Piccadilly to be properly situated within this wider field of debate. In the event a set of rather different questions intruded themselves, questions which had to do with the role which the archive plays is disseminating political memoryscapes.

Ten Days That Shook My World: Remembering 144 Piccadilly between Spectacle and Trauma

In addition to the personal memories they evoked, the objects I brought with me to the MayDay Rooms archive played host to a whole gamut of media myths which are ripe for deconstruction. Rather than treat these materials as relics, ritual objects of commemoration, it seemed more to the point to regard them as agents provocateurs in an emergent network of possible interpretations, clues as to what their still-to-be-figured-out significance might be.

I had in any case already written about the political sociology of the street commune squats and also about its personal impact on me.[20] Whatever claim to social objectivity or biographical authenticity these texts might have, there is still another story waiting to be told whenever the graphic traces of these events are presented to others. The inevitable reframing that takes place in the act of consigning materials ensures that whatever future posterity is achieved for them cannot be reduced to or approximate the significance they may have had in the past. The raw remains of the past may indeed be chaotic and condemned to insignificance, but we should not delude ourselves into thinking that, by retrieving them, they can be returned to some aboriginal meaning.

My first exhibit was not one. My favourite BIFF cartoon was never drawn but it shows a balding lecturer standing in front a group of very bored-looking students, saying, 'Did I ever tell you about the time I spent in a hippy squatter commune in 1968—it was a moment of profound *détournement*, but unfortunately I had my sleeping bag nicked'.[21] Like any urban social movement, the street communes generated their own idiom, their own slogans, their own iconography, if you like their own subculture, although in this case the squats drew in young people of many subcultural allegiances and of none. The Left did not quite know what to make of us. After all we were neither students nor workers. When we turned up at a conference of the Revolutionary Socialist Students Federation (RSSF) at the Roundhouse in Camden Town in the naive belief that we would gain their support for our campaign against police harassment and the 'sus' laws (or 'stop and search' laws), we were quickly thrown out amid shouts of 'What do you produce? Syringes?' The libertarian Left was more accommodating, and there were personal as well as ideological links to the English Situationists grouped around *Heatwave* and *King Mob Echo*. Still, Notting Hill, where the majority of the English 'Situs' were based was a long way from 'the Dilly' in terms of both political and cultural geography. The family squatting movement led by Ron Bailey was likewise quick to dissociate itself from our occupations, worried no doubt that they would be tarred with the same lurid media brush as drop-outs and down-and-outs sponging off the state.[22] The question then is how to locate the material generated by the events within a broader ideological landscape: how does the archive contextualise what is consigned to it, whether by placing a deliberate interpretative frame around it, or simply by its presence there?

My second exhibit was only slightly less imaginary. It consisted of some pages from a novel written about 144 Piccadilly by Samuel Fuller, who had the idea of making a movie about it but perhaps fortunately never did. It would probably have been a cross between the gothic imaginary of *Shock Corridor* and a film noir like *Street of No Return*. In the book, which is based on media reports, only more sexed up, Dr John is played by Robert, a rather earnest, intellectual hippy with pacifist tendencies who goes off the rails. In the movie he would probably have been played by Peter Fonda, of *Easy Rider* fame.

The following excerpt, from the final chapter, gives a flavour of the thing:

> Lover Boy stared at Robert, surprised, and gasped, "You're crazy!"
> In sickening slow motion Lover Boy crumpled backwards and
> lay sprawled under the red tipped sword in Robert's hand. Several

drops of blood fell on Lover Boy's eye patch. The kid with the tattooed cock looked dead. I crawled through darting kicking feet to Lover Boy and in the middle of the ear-shattering fighting I explored with shaky fingers. His one glassy eye stared up at me in frozen shock.

I looked around. No one else had seen the action.

No one!

Above me stood Robert. There was no expression in his face.

Then a voice rose above the confusion. It kept on shouting, over and over again: *"They're coming!"*

It was Girish. *"The cops are coming!"*

Angels fled to defend the squat. Through a window I saw a Scotland Yard commander posting policemen outside 144. About two thousand people were in the crowd. Heavy traffic halted, curious drivers abandoned cars to join the crowd. The police were vainly trying to keep the traffic moving. An Inspector entered the forecourt even as squatters poured across the drawbridge to escape arrest. The Inspector stepped over the heavy chain. Behind him several bobbies approached with drug-sniffing dogs.

The Inspector produced a paper and in a loud voice said, "This is a search warrant under the Dangerous Drugs Act". He was halfway across the drawbridge when the Angels flung him over the rail into the concrete basement below. Whistles shrilled and a wave of police rushed forwards. Immediately they were pelted with a stockpile of missiles. Squatters now gone stark raving mad were continuing the battle.

The Battle of Hippy Castle had begun.[23]

Though the novel was pitched as 'the true inside story of 144', it is clear from the very first page that it is entirely based on the most sensationalist accounts of the tabloid press. Even as a piece of pulp fiction, it is so badly written as to be a disgrace to the genre. But then Fuller was writing a Hollywood movie script, not a work of literature or social documentation.

The question this text raises though is just what kind of spectacle the 144 occupation was and how it should be presented in the archive. The occupation was certainly not consciously conceived as a piece of street theatre performed for the media—unlike the anti–Vietnam War protest staged at the Democratic National Convention in Chicago in 1968 or Weatherman's Days of Rage demonstrations the following year, which from the outset were planned with one eye on media coverage.[24] Yet the building certainly did become a platform on which a whole variety of actors performed: the Hells Angels who provided the security force, the skinheads from East London outside the building who spent their time trading missiles and insults with the Angels, the Beef Steak Society who, contrary to Fuller's account, set up their trenchers in the courtyard and proceeded to enjoy a three-course meal of traditional English fare to make the point that people who worked for a living and paid their taxes could enjoy the good things in life! The balconies in particular served an important function, at once lookout points and a platform from which to see and be seen by the crowds of spectators below. The street communards were certainly not passive victims of corporate media hysteria or innocent of the news impact of a mass squat in a palatial mansion once owned by royalty. The slogan painted across the facade of the building, 'We Are the Writing on Your Walls' unites the performative and the iconographic in a knowing gesture of defiance which both recognises its political fragility and its power of dissemination.

The next exhibit illustrated this dialectic very well. My own personal archive of 144 and the other street commune squats contains cuttings from both the tabloid and broadsheet press, leaflets and other ephemera produced by the London Street Commune, and some photographs. The material is contained in a large dossier about three feet square, with stiff cardboard covers, on which I have written a dedication to my adoptive son Stephen. So it is very much a bit of personal-history-as-legacy. The material is displayed on sheets of brown paper, many of the cuttings have age spotting, and the whole dossier is in a fragile condition. It is a prime candidate for digitisation, which is one reason I decided to deposit it. My decision to locate it in the MayDay Rooms, rather than, say, the Museum of London, was because I wanted the material to find its place within a wider archive of Sixties radicalism rather than be regarded as an exotic addition to mainstream metropolitan history. Yet the nature of the material itself, which mostly consists of highly sensationalised press reportage, poses a particular challenge for a radical Left archive of this kind. The curatorial issue is how to avoid either uncritically reproducing a highly mediatised version of the event via dramatic images, or to 'deconstruct' it in such a way that its existential impact on those who lived through it entirely disappears.

Looking through the press cuttings again I was struck by certain recurrent themes in the way the squat was depicted. There was the trope of 144 as a haunted house, inhabited by drugged-out zombies. And there was the spectre of private property being appropriated and turned over to public ownership thanks to a loophole created by an ancient law and, as such, threatening the very foundations of bourgeois society. Predictably this was the favoured storyline of the Tory press.

Then there was 144 as *Home Alone*, a cautionary tale of what happens when parents are away and the children take over. This was the subtext in much of the liberal press, most notably the *Guardian*, the *Observer* and *New Society*.

Finally there was a positive rendition of this theme in the view of 144 as an alternative orphanage, a place where children and young people flocked to find a home away from home, to break away from repressive family values and experiment with new and more liberating lifestyles. This, of course, was the line taken by the underground press.

The question all this raises for me is how such one-dimensional 'outsider' accounts can be challenged or disrupted without positing some ultimately authentic 'insider' story as their critical counterpoint or support. Perhaps the archive can create a third space, not so much of neutral arbitration, or even dialogue between these two standpoints, as a means of interrogating what is at stake in both.

My next exhibit was a rubber stamp, with 'London Street Commune' engraved on it. We used it at 144 to stamp people's hands as they came and went from the building, rather like what happens in a rave or night club. After the fifth day of the squat only those who could show the mark at the door were allowed in. It was the only way we had of controlling the numbers when these swelled beyond what the building could accommodate as result of all the publicity. This little device was the nearest we came to exercising any kind of direct organisational authority or control over the squat. So here the object itself stands directly for the material practice it made possible, and to handle it, is to simulate our somewhat futile attempt to impose some kind of bureaucratic order onto a chaotic situation. Once located in the archive, however, this item risks rubber-stamping the prevailing view that anarchism is a self-defeating project because it fetishises spontaneity and succumbs to the 'tyranny of structurelessness'. In fact the 144 street commune succeeded in housing and feeding nearly eight hundred quasi-homeless young people for several weeks in a building which was hardly designed as a youth hostel or holiday camp.

My penultimate exhibit was a rubber duck. Or rather *Rubber Duck*, the first and final edition of a newspaper produced by Street Aid, the successor organisation to the London Street Commune, and written largely by ex-street communards. It was aimed at the large floating homeless population of young people in the West End: as well as feature articles, including one about 144 Piccadilly, it included information about hostels, legal rights, and a map of squats, 'derries', and all-night cafes and clubs. It was not exactly *Big Issue*, although we did make some spare cash selling it around the West End.[25] In its rather scruffy layout and design it does convey something of the improvisational spirit of the street communes, and the wild spectrum of viewpoints and concerns which coalesced around the squats. That does not mean this kind of material should be assigned privileged evidential status or exempted from critique. Ephemera, by definition, are produced in the heat of the moment, but this does not make such material more authentic as an expression of political attitude or opinion than more considered statements, merely more difficult to collect and interpret. In fact *Rubber Duck* has to be read in relation to the emergence of a whole new style of underground or alternative journalism in the mid-1960s. An archive of political counter cultures is perhaps the best place to ensure that such a reading is possible.

My final deposition was a photograph and brought together the personal and political aspects of the squat. It is a head-and-shoulders portrait which shows me wearing my 'original' T-shirt caked in oil paint which had become my public fashion statement (I had vowed not to take it off until our demands were met). It was very uncomfortable to wear, more like a hair shirt than a T-shirt, and also very smelly. The photograph was taken by a *Daily Mail* reporter and on the back of it is the following inscription:

Dear Mrs Cohen,
This is the photograph of the man known as Doctor John, who is a leader of the 144 Piccadilly squat and whom we believe to be your son. Can you please positively identify that this is the case. If you would like to contact me I am enclosing my phone number.
(signed) *Daily Mail* Reporter

The photograph had been pushed through the letterbox at my parents' flat in Bloomsbury, whither the reporter had somehow traced me. I do

Dr John

not know how the *Mail* had got wind of my 'real' identity but along with reporters from the *Sun* and *Mirror* they camped out in the downstairs lobby of the block of flats near Euston where my parents lived, perhaps in the hope of getting an 'exclusive' from me, although I had not been home for over a year. Eventually the press harassment got so bad that my parents had to leave town and go to stay with friends in the country.

It must have been quite a shock for my mother to be suddenly confronted with this photograph of her prodigal son. How could she possibly recognise her version of me in the bearded wild man I had apparently become and who represented everything that, as an avid *Daily Mail* reader, she had been told to fear and loathe? According to my father, the public shame she thought my notoriety in the Tory press had brought on the family name was so great that she resigned as a local Tory Councillor. She felt she would be blamed for bringing up a son who had turned out to be Public Enemy Number One and would become an electoral liability to the party. In fact I am sure she would have received a large sympathy vote, but my father never forgave me for having wrecked her bona fide political career in wilful pursuit of my own delinquent one.

Photographs have the capacity to not only freeze-frame a moment in the temporal flux of events, but to yank it out of its immediate context and give it trans-historical significance. Unlike a caption which anchors the meaning of an image to a site-specific narrative, however arbitrarily, an inscription such as the one on the back of my photograph both evokes a primordial issue of recognition—does this mother acknowledge her son and what or who he has become?—and puts in question the very nature of mimetic representation in the age of 'fake news'. How, after all, could this photograph be a 'true likeness' when the persona it depicts was entirely invented by the media as a 'folk devil' in an orchestrated moral panic about deviant and anarchic youth?

There is a historical irony at work here. The photographic archive was pioneered as an apparatus of state surveillance and bureaucratic governance, rendering all mug shots equivalent as instances of depravity or deviance from some statistical norm of citizenship. But in the age of Snapchat and Instagram it has become a platform for a mass culture of narcissism in which millions of selfies vie with one another to affirm an identikit pose of individuality. Under these circumstances the archival task of restoring to the photograph its aura of ambiguity takes on a new urgency.

In summoning up and reflecting on images and texts from the past which have a direct autobiographical reference it is all too easy to view them in the distorting mirror of self-regard. The temptation is even greater when the remembered events evoke principles of hope that have become tenuous or unsustainable in a subsequent political conjuncture. It is not difficult today for Sixties radicals to feel that things have gone backwards, that everything they fought for and sometimes achieved is in danger of being swept away and there will soon be nothing left to mark the impact they once had, except what is archived. Hence the frantic attempts at revivalism, both in Britain and the USA.[26] To at last create a legacy from which there is no turning back!

The power of the archive to exorcise the demons of the past *and* to forge putative links with the present conjuncture is intrinsic to such projects. But it is a tricky operation. We have seen it at work in the retro-chic radicalism prevalent in some of the fiftieth anniversary events organised around May '68, providing a platform for many an erstwhile revolutionary to misrecognise today's 'Generation Rent' as the true inheritors of their own values and ideals. Projective—and retrospective—political identifications often skip a generation; it is always easier to be generous towards one's grandparents' achievements in and against adversity, while blaming one's parents for the unfair advantage which circumstances have bestowed on them, and which they have been unable to pass on as opportunities for their children.

Yet we need to be careful about imputing to the archive a capacity which it may usurp or extend but which exists independently of it, namely the transmission of collective memory. Any significant event, whether archived or not, casts a long shadow over those who have lived through it. The scenes witnessed at 144, many of them undocumented, left an indelible impression on many former street communards and have continued to shape the way they think about politics, culture and society. In the words of one of them, a manual worker and trade unionist who became a housing activist: 'It was not a question of going with or against the tide of history: for a brief moment we *were* the tide'.

It is clearly important to document the quality of such experiences and the forms of solidarity and collective struggle associated with them. At the same time we also have to acknowledge that activist political cultures tend to iterate on a single polemical note and lend themselves to tunnel visions. The real task for any Living Archive of the Left is not to resurrect the past—to reanimate the corpse of 1968 and all that, for example—nor to neatly pigeonhole events and movements according to some a priori schema but rather to capture their *divergence* from the historical context in which they were embedded, to restore to them their futurity, even their counterfactuality, which is also their potential to reconfigure the present.

The swarm of personal associations triggered by the 144 Piccadilly material opened up a series of political questions for me which are as much prospective as retrospective. Was this strange alliance of young dossers or rough sleepers and teenage runaways with beats, hippies, bohemians and radical students an anticipation of what Hardt and Negri have called 'the multitude', a disparate assembly of those living a precarious existence on the margins of capitalism and occupying unregulated pop-up niches in the fabric of the city? Or was it merely a parody of a riotous mob confined to a building, making a media spectacle of itself and distracting attention from the real political issues of the day which had to do with the deindustrialisation of Britain, the beginning of the end of labourism and the manual working class as a major progressive historical force? Such questions are very much part of a present-tense debate about whether or not the Left has a future.[27] Has the Left the capacity to reclaim its political imagination from recuperation and perversion by corporate capitalism? Can its memoryscapes be more and other than an involuntary response to the ruin of those dreams of a better world historically bound up with communism and the labour movement? Is it possible to enunciate realistic principle of hope which articulate popular demands for social justice without falling back into pragmatic opportunism or utopian fantasies?

At a micro-political level we have to consider whether archiving a counter-hegemonic culture requires different methodologies from those which have shaped the conventional historical record. If the archive is not a neutral space but a site of critical engagement and debate, does it mean that its programmatic ambitions necessarily trump whatever aspirations individual donors may have for the material they deposit? Does it mean that material is only donated and collected if it is animated by the same political vision or critical perspective as that of the archivist? To address such issues we need to look in more detail at the contemporary legacy politics of the Left.

In My End Is Others' Beginning: Left Legacy Politics and the Dialectic of Generations

Traditionally the Left has been wedded to the notion that history has lessons to teach us about the present and future. Political defeats, like the UK miners' strike of 1984, for example, should not be ignored or forgotten, because, however painful they yield important insights into how we got to be where we are now. This reflection can sometimes be accompanied by a sense that there is something heroic or even redemptive about a failure if it confirms the existence and overwhelming power of the ruling class. Gramscian pessimism of the intellect can continue to be practised even and especially when optimism of the will has proved disastrous: at least something can be salvaged from the ruins of political hope.[28]

Straw-clutching, which is an occupational hazard *cum* therapy on the left, can sometimes yield interesting results. The outcome of the 1984 miners' strike may have been a disaster for the pit head communities but the unlikely alliance between the hard men of the manual working class and the gay rights movement, as documented in the 2014 film *Pride*, while it does not turn defeat into victory, nevertheless points towards a possible reconfiguration of class and sexual politics which has considerable mileage. Yet there is rarely a simple transformation of bad news into good. This story points back to homoerotic identifications with muscular labouring bodies which have a long history in the problematic relationship of the intelligentsia to the manual working class. Archive that, comrade![29]

For those of us who have lost faith in historical laws and teleologies of any kind to secure ultimate victory, the pressure to find some anchorage, however unstable, for our political affiliations and hopes takes on an urgent existential edge. Knowing that it is very unlikely we will see anything approximating our political vision come to pass in our time, and surrounded on all sides by doom-laden scenarios, it is fatally easy to see our own limited horizon of possibility as the end of the story. What after all have we to leave behind to the next generation, except a litany of failure and defeat? Is it better to leave nothing than to inspire false hopes?

Perhaps the most fundamental human distinction is between those who are simply deceased, whose deaths accomplish nothing but the cessation of life—there is little or nothing of note to remember, few to grieve— and those who leave behind a substantive legacy and hence achieve some kind of afterlife, whether of local or global proportions. For activists who have dedicated their lives to fighting for social justice but who, in their later years, see the tide of history turn against them, the approach of death poses some special legacy issues.[30] Under these circumstances, the drive to archive, to construct a little ark of political covenant in the hope that at some future date, it may be opened under more hospitable circumstances, is correspondingly intense. The archive becomes home to a profoundly cryogenic project.

Yet legacies are never a simple matter of transmission, for there are two contrary processes at work here. The deceased's memory effects may be scattered along with their ashes, as so many individual bequests distributed to family and friends. And then, in a move to preempt or foreclose that process of dispersal, these same effects may be concentrated or reassembled in some kind of archive, to perpetuate the memory and consolidate the reputation. The archive here is literally an ark, a container designed to protect precious objects associated with a life; their donation is a letting go of the material props of memory work while holding on to their symbolic significance. At the same time the legacy archive tends to be part of a wider hagiographical enterprise committed to securing and promoting the reputation of the deceased, or at least to ensuring that their public standing is not subject to critical revision. Yet paradoxically the creation of a legacy out of a life always entails a radical transformation of its meaning; the chain of associations which hitherto connected all these disparate items into a singular life history is replaced by an objective system of archival classification using themes and topics which serve as mnemonic devices quite independently of their original matrix of autobiographical significance. In other words archiving replaces socially grounded memory work and its conversational media with exteriorised, and increasingly digitised, forms of mnemo-technology which merely simulates their impact.[31] Where the material is political, rather than personal, there is a similar displacement effect: the passion accompanying actual events, the sound and the fury of battle, become subdued into the institutional hush of the reading room. Political emotion once re-collected in archival tranquillity does not easily yield up its poetics, unless the quest to dispel the fog of class or culture wars is accompanied by an equally determined commitment to practice the interpretive art 'of being in uncertainties, mysteries, doubts, without any irritable reaching after fact and reason.'

Any act of archival consignment involves a rite of passage which entails a symbolic death, removing the traces of a life or an event from the world which sustained it and secreting them in a special place, a kind of crypt where they are coded and reborn in the form of a public document. This process of encryption, which occurs in both the analog and digital archive, can be a medium of consecrated memory, but it also has the potential to encourage Keats's 'negative capability'.

Such transubstantiations are resisted in cultures where the past is still primarily conveyed through oral tradition and secured by collectively enacted rituals of commemoration; their supersession by virtual technologies should not however be taken for granted. If personality cults rarely survive the death of their subjects, as Adorno sardonically reminds us, less florid myths of personal origin and destiny continue to flourish in the blogosphere. This should lead us to question the all too easy assumption that authenticity lies solely on the side of anamnesis, or that the advent of prosthetic mnemo-technology (hypomnesis) only provides a degraded or surrogate form of memory work.

It is worth noting here that in cultures where oral tradition secures posthumous identity the practice of burying or burning the most precious of the deceased's personal effects along with their mortal remains is widespread. It is a paradoxical form of symbolic action designed to forestall the dispersal of an inheritance by means of a collectively witnessed form of destruction. The ritual marks the moment in which the distinction between the human subject and its objects, so often blurred, becomes dreadfully transparent as the living body is transformed into a corpse which contains nothing but its own putrefaction and the petrified memories of the bereaved. In my view these ceremonies, which make a bonfire of human vanities, represent an unconscious recognition that there is something in the meaning of a life and its loss which is beyond the hubristic reach of the archive and is best consigned to the flames.[32] We shall examine the implications of this for the budding archivee later, but for the moment let us consider its bearing on legacy politics. For the secular Left, death has often been an occasion for the reaffirmation of ideological faith. The end of my struggle marks the beginning of others; the torch is handed on. The funerals of fallen comrades create real as well as imagined communities of mourners around them, and sometimes, of course, they turn into mass demonstrations in which a sense of outrage is tempered by feelings of loss. At other times, the slogan 'don't mourn, organise' becomes the *mot d'ordre*, and displays of anger foreclose the experience of grief or transform it into grievance. Recently the concept of 'active mourning' has emerged in an attempt to find a new equilibrium between the extremes of being immobilised by loss and throwing oneself into political struggle as a manic defence against its recognition. Active mourning is about finding some kind of emotional balance between grief and anger through identification with both the victim and the cause he or she died for.[33]

Where a death is directly politicised, its meaning is utterly transformed, it becomes a public event and to that extent immediate family and friends can come to feel they are even further separated from the deceased *and* from their own feelings. It is not death that has taken their beloved from them so much as the manner of its mourning. In certain extreme cases where martyrology is an essential dynamic, death becomes a chronicle foretold and is actively pledged, if not willed, by the person concerned as a necessary sacrifice for the Cause. But this is not the only possible outcome. The protracted campaigns launched by next of kin, driven by the desire to ensure that the victim of injustice did not die in vain, are

25

Don't Mourn, Organise

one way of preempting or countering this alienation effect.[34] The after-blows of a traumatic death are deflected outwards to its putative cause: the brutal actions of an oppressive state, the class enemy, corrupt or indifferent authority, racial hatred or religious bigotry. In this way the deceased takes on a special posthumous identity intimately implicated in struggles in which they may (or may not) have actually engaged but to which their afterlife is now dedicated.

Full-fledged martyrology, as in the case of Bobby Sands, the IRA hunger striker, does however require some prospective investment on the part of the movements to which the subjects belong.[35] The use of photographs of children injured or killed in a war zone in order to demonstrate the inhumanity of enemies and win sympathy may seem like a cynical manipulation, and at one level it is, but in situations where whole communities are under attack and have mobilised in collective self-defence, no one's life or death is their own. Under such extreme circumstances it may be justified to elide the archival and the political project. Yet as soon as that accommodation hardens into an orthodoxy underpinned by obligatory rituals of collective remembrance, as soon as the archive ceases to be open to improvisation or revision, it becomes part of a more or less oppressive regime of legacy politics.

The underlying idea of history as an *inheritance*, a legacy to be bequeathed by one generation to the next, whether as asset or liability, remains rooted in powerful patriarchal constructs of cultural transmission.[36] Yet it comes up against another equally powerful idea—history as a story of incremental *progress*, in which the past is judged against the present and found wanting. How much more enlightened we are today than our Victorian or Edwardian forebears, how much less sexist, or racist! This rather smug whiggish historicism can also, of course, be reversed. The present is then judged from the vantage point of the past and found to be wanting. Today, large sections of the British Left mourn the legacy it has lost, the world of working-class solidarities, brass bands, the Miners' Gala, industrial ballads, impossibly close-knit homogeneous communities.[37] The Left has developed its own style of melancholia in counterpoint to post-imperial yearnings. In times and places dominated by reactionary values, nostalgia can be a way of holding onto 'core values'; a whole heritage industry has been built around the retrieval and preservation of these now defunct cultures of manual labourism in museums and archives. It is a magical way of laying claim to an inheritance to which there is no longer any apprenticeship. Wrenched out of the economic context which gave them a reason to exist, these cultures tend to become the object of either romantic idealisation, patronising judgement or radical disavowal. Meanwhile outside the museum and the archive, manual workers find themselves written out of the contemporary political script, condemned to a liminal existence as a footnote in a history that has migrated elsewhere.[38]

This preliminary discussion leads us into a series of further questions. How, looking back, in order to look forward, do we estimate the legacy of the campaigns and struggles in which we were personally involved with any kind of objectivity? Is our experience really likely to be of any value or relevance to our children and grandchildren? Of course we must hope that the answer is yes, and struggle to make it so, but we cannot ignore the dialectic of generations to which Marx first drew our attention in *The German Ideology*: 'History is nothing but the succession of separate generations, each of which exploits the materials, the capital formation, the productive forces handed down to it by all the preceding generations, and this on the one hand continues the traditional activity in completely changed circumstances and on the other modifies the old circumstances with completely changed activity'.

So if history is regarded as a kind of inheritance or legacy handed down from one generation to the next, it is also, according to Marx, a transmission which is interrupted by history itself. In my view a generation is a special kind of imagined community based on inventing shared traditions linked to formative experiences of a particular historical conjuncture—1968 or 1989, for example.[39] The sense of belonging to a generation may be very present tense, especially where coming-of-age stories coincide with the emergence of disruptive social forces and cultural practices, so that existential predicaments take on a wider and more collective meaning. But the lived time of 'generationality' is split, continually oscillating between a prospective horizon of shared adventure and a more or less nostalgic re-creation of that time through collective memory work. And because each 'generation' is busily engaged in inventing its own traditions to mark its advent as a historical subject, it tends to ignore or reject the no less invented traditions of its predecessors. There are no 'generational cycles' in history, and 'generation' in itself is an ideological or cultural construct which only in very special circumstances becomes a social or economic force in its own rite. When age cohorts speak and act as if they represent a generation for and to itself, this is usually in order to create a platform from which to mobilise a form of oedipal politics against particular power blocs where these are associated with the exercise of patriarchal authority and an ancien regime.[40]

Of course, there are contexts where all manner of identifications and solidarities occur spontaneously, typically in times of national emergency or war, when people are thrown together by a shared dependency on basic human mutual aid for survival in a way that cuts across existing social divisions such as age, gender, ethnicity or class. In more 'normal', which is to say more rancorous times, it can become the special mission of archives dedicated to the public record of such moments of national unity to re-build these bridges, though usually not without a lot of pontification. It is interesting to note that in the archives devoted to the home front in the Second World War, which certainly do stress the conflict's unifying impact, as well as its liberating effect on women's role as the backbone of the workforce, there is scarcely any mention of wartime socialism, or of the long aftermath of trauma among the cohort of 'blitz kids' who survived the bombing of British cities, and who turned into the angry young men and women of the late 1950s.[41]

Certainly the notion that one generation holds the world in trust for its successors is an attractive one, and one that the environmental movement has made much of. But history-as-legacy may come to be perceived as a poisoned chalice; the younger generation blames its elders for having made such a mess of things, while they in turn blame the young for failing to pick up the torch and carry on their struggle. In some cases, as James Joyce has Stephen Dedalus say in *Ulysses*, 'history is a nightmare from which I am struggling to awake'. Nationalisms, especially subordinated nationalisms, are notorious for imposing old heads on young shoulders and not surprisingly such a burden of representation is often shrugged off. There are too many archives which in the name of preserving cultural heritage or keeping the collective memory of past injustice alive dedicate themselves to the task of legitimating irredentist claims or reviving ancient feuds. In these situations the collective memory becomes weaponised and the archival project is motivated by the desire to settle old scores. Better to forget and move on, let the dead bury the dead in a spirit of reconciliation rather than make the quest for historical truth an accomplice for the reopening of old wounds and engaging in protracted memory wars.[42]

In the case of atrocities, torture, war crimes, ethnic cleansing and genocide, where attempts may have been made to systematically destroy the evidence, along with the human being who might bear witness, the power of the archive's capacity to unearth the hidden and document the obscene comes into its own in tackling the forces of disavowal. Yet there are more subtle resistances at work in obstructing the truth. Collective trauma often seals events in public silence or private symptomatology.[43] Moreover as the phenomenon of 'dark tourism' shows, the archive can find itself complicit in the dissemination of victimologies which become the object of perverse identifications across the generations, as well as fuelling revanchist political claims.[44]

The 'dark' archive, like the negative monument, with its focus on death, loss and catastrophe may provide a much needed counterpoint to the celebratory archive, but as an instrument of mourning or expiation, the graphic detailing of atrocity stories may also leave us feeling helpless in our identification with other people's suffering, an identification which can bring its own, usually disavowed, sadomasochistic pleasures. Certainly audiovisual archives which provide the visitor with an immersive experience of horrific and tragic events need to find ways of framing the material so that it neither reproduces the original trauma and the numbing response nor forces people to dissociate themselves from what is depicted to protect their sense of hope.

Equally the impulse to recover the full existence of communities subject to genocidal attack, however laudable, can lead to archival strategies which cover over the resulting erasures of collective memory and hence minimise the impact. But there is an alternative. One of the most moving and memorable representations of the impact of the Holocaust is to be found in the Jewish Museum in Vienna. In the entrance lobby there is a glass case displaying two telephone directories of the city, both open at the same alphabetical page. One is dated 1936 and the other 1946. At first sight they appear identical, and in format they indeed are. But when you look more closely you see that the pre-*Anschluss* edition contains several hundred Cohens, and ten years later there is not a single Cohen listed. It is by showing what it does not and cannot contain that the archive can bear witness to events whose horror defies adequate representation, and provide a platform for transmitting a legacy of loss to a new generation in a way they can grasp.

Just round the corner from the Jewish Museum, there is another response, even more evocative of absence. Rachel Whiteread's Holocaust Memorial consists of a sealed archive, a concrete mausoleum, whose doors are closed and whose outer walls are lined with casts of books, their spines turned inward, as if arranged by a mad librarian determined that no one shall be able to know their titles, or open their pages to find out what they contain. At one level this monument marks the indestructible nature of Jewish culture, which survived all the Nazis' book burnings to affirm the testimonial power of the word; but also in its aura of frozen stillness, it closure around emptiness, Whiteread's installation resists archival reframing, insisting instead on the involuntary persistence of collective memory across generations, against the genocidal project of the 'final solution'.[45]

Fortunately this is only one side of the legacy story. In more benign circumstances, there is an altogether more positive dialectic at work as historical generations pass each other, like Hegel's old mole, burrowing away in blind pursuit of their own direction home. It is left to historians to make mountains out of the mounds of texts and images they deposit in the cultural landscape. It is then the task of the archivist both to scale the heights of these accumulated interpretations *and* dig beneath their surface contours to unearth the traces of the intellectual journeys invisibly connecting them.

Winners and Losers

We are used to the idea that the winners produce the dominant historiography and that an alternative history—a history of the underdogs, the losers, the people whose voices and lives have been marginalised or suppressed—is nevertheless possible and can be worked up into a counter-hegemonic narrative. This history from below, which E.P. Thomson famously characterised as rescuing these groups from 'the enormous condescension of posterity', can be dramatically counterposed to the top-down history which features the rich and powerful, the big battalions.[46] Yet these two perspectives perhaps share more common ground than their protagonists would like to allow. In both cases there is a common and common-sense notion of history as a zero-sum game, in which every gain is at someone else's expense, in which the only possible outcome is either victory or defeat, one person's profit is another's direct loss. Yet this form of accountancy is only applicable in certain circumstances, which we rightly refer to as turning points or tipping points, or revolutionary moments, to which a bifurcated notion of historical process does indeed correspond. More usually it is a story of mediation, compromise, some partial gains and losses, muddling through.

There is a strong tendency in leftist culture, glossed in Gramsci's famous injunction, to split hearts and minds, will power and knowledge power, political practice and critical theory into separate domains of activity, and in the process to oscillate between unrealistic optimism and abject defeatism.[47] The Left is very good at constructing worst-case scenarios; catastrophism is its default mode. Anyone who has ever done time in

Trotskyite la-la land will know the seductive appeal of the Great Boot in the Sky which appears every time the workers raise their banners high only to be crushed under the heel of the crypto-fascist state or betrayed by their own leaders. But this depressive position is immediately countered by a manic denial of harsh political realities, the affirmation of ultimate triumph. Prophecies of doom give way to a New Dawn, Cenotaph is followed by Jubilee as night follows day.

As a result of this bipolar tendency, the cadences of the Left's historiography tend to get written and remembered all on one note, alternately high or low. Yet it does not have to be this way. Frederic Rzewski's pianistic anthem 'The People United Will Never be Defeated' consists of thirty-five variations on the opening theme, in which it is played hopefully, relentlessly, impatiently, gently, improvisationally, crisply, tenderly, evenly, recklessly and 'like fragments of an absent melody'.[48] To retrieve and represent the rich modulation of feeling mobilised by the Left's political project, especially in its more generous impulses, is surely one of the most urgent tasks and difficult challenges facing its archivists.

Moreover, to assume that history-as-success story is confined to institutions, groups or individuals with wealth and power is clearly wrong. Cultural history, the history of ideas, the history of science is full of movers and shakers who were outsiders, and definitely not part of any 'establishment'; they succeeded against all the odds in changing the rules of the game. And as we will see below this has a direct bearing on the changing apparatus of fame, celebrity and the brokerage of 'immortality'.

When it comes to popular history, to popular democratic struggles, like Peterloo and the Chartists, the Paris Commune, the 1926 General Strike, the Spanish Civil War, the postwar miners strikes, independence and national liberation struggles, the poll tax riots, and so on, when we look at how these big moments are portrayed in films, on TV, in historical novels, and how such events become sedimented in the collective memory of a society or particular protagonists within it, then we see the game of winners and losers being played for much higher stakes. And so the temptation to play 'loser wins'—to conjure retrospective victory out of the bitter ashes of defeat—is correspondingly high.

According to the subtle dialectics of Marxist-Leninism such games of 'loser wins' are a self-defeating strategy. But this principle has its roots in the crude thoughts of common-sense culture, as Brecht may have indeed been aware: everyone wants to be on the winning side of history. The point was brought home to me when I had to teach history to a group of stroppy teenage school truants from a local council estate in Covent Garden which was under threat from a large regeneration scheme.[49] Their interest in the past was confined to last year's top-ten hits, and the record of Arsenal in the FA cup, about which topics they were very knowledgeable. I decided to do a series of lessons about action-packed events in which there was a clash of contending social and ideological forces leading to a dramatic outcome: the 1381 Peasants' Revolt and the Kronstadt sailors' uprising were two of my main case studies. This was in the naive belief that their imaginations would be captured by the sheer excitement of it all, and their sympathy with the underdogs stirred by the heroic but doomed resistance of peasants and workers. Perhaps they would make the connection between these past struggles and their parents own fight against corporate capitalism? Not a bit of it. As one of the boys put it, when I asked what could be learnt from the Peasants' Revolt: 'They lost, Sir, didn't they'. Growing up in a culture in which the playground taunt of 'loser' touches the most hidden wounds of class, knowing that they had already been written off by the education system as losers, these boys were desperate for quick wins. They had no time for the *longue durée*, for the idea that the Peasants' Revolt, for all its failure, marked the beginning of the end of feudal absolutism.

Now it so happens that in *The Poverty of Philosophy*, his withering critique of Proudhon's facile historicism, Marx uses the case of feudalism to suggest another version of winners and losers. He writes:

> Feudalism had two antagonistic elements which are designated by the name of the good side and the bad side of feudalism, irrespective of the fact that it is always the bad side that in the end triumphs over the good side. It is the bad side that produces the movement which makes history, by providing a struggle. If, during the epoch of the domination of feudalism, the economists, enthusiastic over the knightly virtues, the beautiful harmony between rights and duties, the patriarchal life of the towns, the prosperous condition of domestic industry in the countryside, the development of industry organized into corporations, guilds and fraternities, in short, everything that constitutes the good side of feudalism, had set themselves the problem of eliminating everything that cast a shadow on the picture—serfdom, privileges, anarchy—what would

have happened? All the elements which called forth the struggle would have been destroyed, and the development of the bourgeoisie nipped in the bud. One would have set oneself the absurd problem of eliminating history.

We know that the latter-day advocates of the 'end of history' do indeed see capitalism as a success story in these terms: it is the only game in town and its destructiveness, its bad side, is just an unfortunate but necessary facet of its dynamic creativity. Joseph Schumpeter's reformulation travesties Marx's profound insight into the central contradiction of capitalism, namely that capital could not produce wealth without also reproducing poverty, and that its drive to replace living, value creating, labour power with technology or dead labour, to increase productivity, if that project were ever to be fully achieved, would result in its own demise. Schumpeter turned that tragic contradiction into a simple contrary, a Hegelian paradox, in which the expropriation, perversion or elimination of any mode of production other than its own, was the price a minority had to pay for the benefits which capitalism brought the vast majority.[50] In so doing he opened the door to the traditional liberal standpoint which sees good and bad in everything.

Yet if we hold to the classical Marxist view that history proceeds solely by its bad side, by its negative dialectic, we can quickly find ourselves mired in a morally unsustainable position. Do we really wish for the further immiseration of the poor in the futile hope that it will transform them into a force capable of overthrowing capitalism? Do we ransack history in the quest for ever-more-numerous instances of black oppression, working-class exploitation, the persecution of the Jews, the discrimination against women and children, in order to join them up into a grand narrative of heroic popular resistance to adversity in the belief that this will somehow bring about the fire next time? There are plenty of archives devoted to this worthy proposition, but unfortunately they tend to produce somewhat blinkered views of history.

Communist parties, whether in power or in opposition, have always been assiduous archivists *and* tunnel visionaries. The party apparatchiks regarded History as the supreme arbiter of the value of their actions; yet at the same time they never entirely trusted the 'laws of motion' which orthodox Marxism depicts as the hidden hand guiding concrete historical development. History as *longue durée*, if not *sub specie aeternitatis*, may be without guarantees, but for orthodox Marxists it is also without surprises, because the conceptual apparatus of historical materialism allows for a multiplicity of outcomes without making its validity dependent on any one of them. It is to protect party ideology against this uncertainty principle that the archive is mobilised to impose a regime of truth on the empirical historical record and to discredit or suppress alternative narratives which challenge its hegemony. This may, of course, involve deliberate acts of falsification, but in any case these are rationalised in archival protocols that filter out any disturbing material as a matter of bureaucratic course. Yet, paradoxically, once History is regarded as both a teleology without foundation and a tribunal whose judgments are magically free from the gravitational pull of actual events, the archive as such becomes redundant, its place taken by cultural memory of permanent equivocation. Let us not forget Fidel Castro, who in his famous speech in defence of the action at the Moncada Barracks declared to the court that 'history will absolve me' but when asked many years later what he thought was the world-historical significance of the French Revolution replied that 'it is still too early to tell'.

This deep ambivalence towards the historical process and hence to the archival project as its underpinning, was first noted by Marx in a famous passage in the *Eighteenth Brumaire of Louis Napoleon*, where he once again embeds it in the dialectic of generations:

> Men make their own history, but they do not make it as they please; they do not make it under self-selected circumstances, but under circumstances existing already, given and transmitted from the past. The tradition of all dead generations weighs like a nightmare on the brains of the living. And just as they seem to be occupied with revolutionizing themselves and things, creating something that did not exist before, precisely in such epochs of revolutionary crisis they anxiously conjure up the spirits of the past to their service, borrowing from them names, battle slogans, and costumes in order to present this new scene in world history in time-honoured disguise and borrowed language.

There are notable examples of archives being mobilised to provide this kind of historical anchorage for the creation of grand narratives of epochal change. And not only on the left. The time signature of Marx's formula can be reversed and the past made to sing a descant to the future as principle of continuity, not rupture. For example, Alexandr Sokurov's film

Russian Ark takes us on a journey through the Hermitage Museum in Saint Petersburg in a single, continuous travelling shot following an imaginary French Marquis as he goes on a rambling tour of this monument to the cultural heritage of Russia's governing elite from the seventeenth century to 1917. The museum is indeed an ark which has protected an aristocratic sense of Russian identity more or less untouched by war, revolution and the other calamities of the twentieth century. This is meat and drink to a new generation of Russian narodniki who have adorned their populism with this aristocratic carapace in order to oppose the born-again nomenklatura and their policy of replacing the economic shackles of Communism with the worst aspects of neoliberal capitalism, under the watchful eye of an authoritarian state. Sokurov subverts this nationalist/populist rhetoric with its dressing up of the future in the clothes of the past, by inserting a counter-narrative, a whispered interior dialogue in which the Marquis expresses bewilderment at finding himself adrift in time.

This pervasive sense of temporal dislocation is one of the consequences of the fall of Soviet Communism. Its effect has been to liberate popular memory in the Eastern Bloc countries from the dead weight of several generations of official commemoration and to restore to the archive its subversive, revisionary power.[51] In the exemplary work of Svetlana Alexievich, and especially in her book *Secondhand Time* (2013), we see how oral history can be used to illuminate the impact which profound structural changes have on the everyday lives of ordinary people by focusing on intimate personal details and the tense ambiguities of their response to events going on around them in which they may be willingly or unwillingly caught up.

Such accounts defy pigeonholing as 'for' or 'against' the historical process they depict. Alexievich's book reveals the tragic—and sometimes comic—circumstances of growing up within the Soviet regime at the time of its final collapse. In the West, liberals and many on the left have welcomed the book as demonstrating the survival of a popular spirit of resistance to Stalinism and its long aftermath. It was tempting to recruit her work for the view that every historical event and political movement is at once progressive and reactionary, leaving it to posterity to judge the final balance of forces. This approach, having it both ways, is popular with many archivists, who do not want to be accused of bias and feel that the implied relativism of showing multiple interpretations of the same event is anyway epistemologically de rigueur. Welcome to the Museum of

Dialectical Idealism. Like postmodernism itself, with its cult of the 'unreliable narrator', I think this is a bit of a cop out. But what kind of standpoint, moral and epistemological, can we construct which does not rest on some a priori claim to value neutrality or undecidability, never mind 'objectivity', yet still enables the political archive, in all its inevitable selectivity of materials, to avoid becoming the site of endless ideological battles which may tear it apart?

Let Us Now Praise Famous People: Paradigms of Remembrance and the Twin Cultures of Modernity

One way to grasp what is at stake here is to consider the underlying grammars of the historical imagination, the different ways there are of articulating past, present and future into a narratable and hence archivable memoryscape, what Bakhtin called a 'chrono-topography'.[52] The first grammar we might call *proto-modernist* and is indeed about the constant process of modernisation linked to advances in science and technology, and to developmental ideals for both society and the self premised on the notion of *progress*.[53] Within this frame, the past is what is left behind by the present as it progresses into the future as its open horizon of possibility. The past only returns as what has been forgotten or repressed in the pursuit of progress and is retrieved by the intervention of some special mnemonic device where it appears as a principle of continuity—the plan or law or higher purpose which governs the unfolding of processes in historical time. Within this frame the momentum of progress appears to be self-generated and unstoppable, and it is usually linked to an optimistic or redemptive vision of the future. Proto-modernism continually creates new prototypes of modernity; each instance of 'the modern' functions as a metonym within the wider discourse of modernity. For the proto-modernist the archive offers a privileged prospect on an ever-changing world. Proto-modernists have become great devotees of material culture and the cargo cults of consumerism, but they are also fully paid up members of the throwaway society. Objects and their associated memories that are deemed to be past their sell-by date are either updated or, failing that, binned and replaced by more recent acquisitions. Proto-modern archivists are unsentimental in their approach to collecting and are always on the lookout for some new trend to document.

In many radical academic circles today, especially those influenced by postmodernist paradigms, this model is pretty much discredited along with the Enlightenment Ideal and the Whig interpretation of history with which it is associated. But it is very much alive in popular historiography where it sustains social aspirations and social movements of every kind, especially those linked with identity politics. Proto-modernists, by definition, practice optimism of the will. People who have inherited a lot of intellectual and cultural capital tend to be rather snooty about this form of popular historicism, perhaps because the do-it-yourself heritage industry builds cultural capital and anchors it in *lieux de mémoire* outside the academy, including in those little archives of souvenir objects, images and texts collected as building blocks for autobiographies that will never be written. I would argue that under favourable circumstances this form of archival practice can help build the internal resources of resilience needed to sustain struggles of long duration, where defeats can be regarded as only temporary setbacks, blips in the onward march to a better future. But by the same token, Left proto-modernism remains complicit with or subordinate to the dominant liberal ideology of progress, in particular the view that advances in public understanding inevitably lead to greater social justice. This provides the archive with a beguiling script organised around a timeline documenting the advances made towards greater social equality through particular struggles: a vital correction to the official public record, according to which such progress is made solely by enlightened politicians and policymakers. But the intervention remains at the level of archival content rather than form.

Let us take a concrete example of this problem. Adoption history is usually produced within the framework of child welfare or family law. Once located there it tends to form part of grand narrative of institutional progress, in which a straight line is traced from the bad old days, associated with the foundling hospital, the orphanage, and the stigma of illegitimacy, to the good new days where a state of enlightenment prevails, in terms of current policy, provision and public attitude.[54] The altruism of Child Rescue is often made the main motivating force in this onward march, allowing little room for discontinuity or reversal. History is simply not supposed to proceed by its 'bad side'. This model is all the more seductive in that it mirrors a positivism in which the authorised version of the adoption story was inscribed until quite recently: the child was supposed to move forward from bad beginnings, associated with the birth parents, to happy endings linked to the adoptive parents, and this progress was measured by the extent to which the past was left behind and the present lived as an open horizon of future possibility. It was to protect the adopted child from knowledge of a disruptive past that the official adoption archive, containing case reports, correspondence and other documents, remained off limits until the child was eighteen. The closed archive actively suppressed the desire to know about beginnings. For generations of adopted children, opening the archive thus became a bizarre rite of passage into adulthood which problematised their whole sense of identity as it put them in touch with their origins.[55]

Against this background, the investigation of adoptee life histories has been largely carried out by people seeking to uncover the circumstances leading to the adoption and thereby retrieve some sense of their lost inheritance. This work, pursued until recently in the face of official discouragement or indifference, necessarily took the form of a genealogical project: the unfolding of a hidden principle of difference which was constitutive of the subject's identity. This research is also often described in archaeological terms—digging away to uncover traces of lost childhoods buried under layers of adult misrepresentation. Quite spontaneously these little do-it-yourself archives offer an alternative to official teleologies of progress, albeit often through a narrative coloured by the family romance and its narrative of fictive kinship.[56] For in the case of adoptees, the phantasy of having been 'kidnapped' by the people who are bringing you up and of belonging to a quite different and far more glamorous or exotic parentage corresponds quite closely to the real situation, albeit transposed into the idiom of wish fulfilment. Although apparently subversive of the official adoption story, this myth of origins conserves the basic plot line in an inverted form; it is underwritten by the fanciful belief that the child will be discovered and reclaimed by its 'real' (i.e., idealised because absent) birth parents and will live happily ever after in a world where everything has been made magically better. The adoption archive supports this construct only in so far as it remains a pure imaginary space where the child will one day be restored to its once-upon-a-time grandiose status. So what begins as a project of '*détournement*', liberating the archival format from its repressive institutional mechanism of silence, ends with 'recuperation', providing a platform for the reassertion of welfare progressivism by adoptive children themselves as they are reunited with birth parents in phantasy, an outcome which will make any encounter in the real world all the more difficult and even traumatic.

As this example shows, proto-modernism is closely entailed in the notion of historical progress as an inevitable and incremental step-by-step change for the betterment of the human condition—greater tolerance, less everyday violence, better health, longer life spans etc. Within this frame, for example, the history of disciplines is written as one of progress towards ever-greater knowledge and understanding, and this Enlightenment narrative is inscribed in their propaedeutics. Yet this idea of progress is everywhere in crisis. Increasingly progress has come to mean the simple intensification or acceleration of present trends into the future and indeed there is a whole discourse of 'futurology' built on this extrapolation.[57] But what kind of progress is it that today more people in affluent Western societies die from eating too much than from starvation and more commit suicide than are murdered?

The crisis of progress has opened up a second chrono-topography which might be called *retro-modernist*, in the sense that it regards modernity not as something to be aimed at or achieved but as something that has never quite happened, is basically unachievable and can only be grasped as a kind of retro-fit.[58] Here the present is experienced and narrated as a discontinuous series of discrete moments, belonging to an often chaotic synchronicity, split off from a past which never fades but continues to be re-presented and recycled, and from a future which is blocked, occluded, threatening or unimaginable. History is now decomposed into a series of unconnected moments, mashed up into a more or less spectacular collage of fragments. Within this frame, modernity is never fully present to itself; it is represented by its avatars or through a play of metaphoric substitutions. By definition, retro-modernists practice pessimism of the intellect.

At one level, then, this perspective involves a profound dehistoricising of experience, a radical disconnect between past, present and future. It amortises intellectual and cultural capital, which decreases in value over time and, if unchecked, hollows out the cognitive and emotional resources needed to sustain struggles of long duration. It can also foreclose the scope and scale of collective memoryscapes which might support meaningful archiving. For example, in the teaching of the arts and humanities, students no longer learn to interrogate the history of their disciplines, that is all yesterday's news, at best telescoped into a superficial 'back story' without any intellectual or emotional hinterland. Instead, lacking any form of apprenticeship to a viable inheritance, their work is driven by a restless quest for authenticity, if only one rooted in its immediate mode of production which is endlessly archived in footnotes, in ever-more-ritualistic displays of academic scholarship.

Fortunately this is only one side of the story. Retro-modernism also opens up a space for re-historicising the social imaginary, for the creation of retro-chic cultures as well as the projection of, usually dystopian, futures. Retro-modernists are great hoarders of objects and their archives often create nostalgic evocations of lost worlds of modernity that can be recycled for ever new times.

Nostalgia is one of the great drivers of archive fever and is often associated with kitsch.[59] One of the most pernicious effects of kitsch is to corrupt nostalgia, to deprive it of its authentic melancholic properties, by converting the painful sense of loss or dislocation into a yearning for a cosy form of homeliness, embodied in familiar objects, in a return to a world that never existed in the first place. Parting is always a sentimental occasion and a prompt for memory work, but it should be sentimentality with depth or, as Ernst Bloch more accurately describes it, 'a tremolo hovering indistinguishably between surface and depth'.[60]

The archival project similarly hovers between an impossible retrieval of the lost object and its pseudo-reproduction. For retro-modernists are not just passéists; they are just as nostalgic for the future. In fact by liberating the archival imagination from empirical constraint, the retro-modernist project sometimes makes it possible to think the unthinkable and even represent it. For example, Orhan Pamuk's Museum of Innocence, based on his novel of the same name, consists of an extended archive of the narrator's wanderings through old Istanbul in search of material traces of a lost lover.[61] A barrette, a salt shaker she once touched, the little china dog that sits on top of her family's television, souvenirs of places they visited together, a table mat from the cafe where they used to meet, photographs, all these objects find their home in the museum, assembled in cabinets of curiosity in a way which requires a narrative key to unlock their meaning, supplied by the novel itself.

This is an archive of lost opportunity and regrets in pursuit of love and happiness. It portrays Istanbul as a post-imperial city that has never quite achieved modernity, at least not in its Western form, but which remains a living monument to its own better days. It is as if, unthinkably, the Ataturk modernisers, with their vision of Turkey's future as a secular state, had only succeeded in re-creating the aura of the Ottoman Empire without its power. There is nothing kitsch about the Museum

The Museum of Innocence

of Innocence; the displays exude an authentic melancholia, a nostalgia for what was once upon a time a shared but now impossible vision of the future. For Pamuk, as for many retro-modernists, the archive is indeed a refuge from the storm of progress presided over by the angel of history which Walter Benjamin famously described in these terms:

> His face is turned toward the past. Where we perceive a chain of events, he sees one single catastrophe which keeps piling wreckage upon wreckage and hurls it in front of his feet. The angel would like to stay, awaken the dead, and make whole what has been smashed. But a storm is blowing from Paradise; it has got caught in his wings with such violence that the angel can no longer close them. This storm irresistibly propels him into the future to which his back is turned, while the pile of debris before him grows skyward. This storm is what we call progress.[62]

Whether proto- or retro-modernist in orientation, the latent function of the archive is to tackle the sense of temporal dislocation that is the ever-emergent feature of modernity, and to do so by positing and guaranteeing a future to come. That is one reason why the archive is increasingly enrolled to serve as an apparatus of fame. The posthumous future which it makes possible does not consist of empty homogeneous time punctuated by postmortem anniversaries, nor is it a site of pure indeterminacy, whether split off and opposed to the present or emergent from it. Rather, the archive maps a trajectory of meaning that holds out the possibility of bringing the dead back to life. As such, archive fever can indeed be interpreted as a manic defence against the death instinct, shoring up our self-importance against a pervasive sense that even in the short run most of us are condemned to oblivion, a fact daily impressed on us by the accelerated obsolescence of the 'identity goods' in which we so often invest our hopes and memories. By the same token archival projects are often mobilised to reanimate dead ideologies, artificially prolonging the life of ideas well past their sell-by date and resurrecting the memory of people who have been, quite justly, consigned to the dustbins of history.

A good case in point is the revival of interest, even idolatry, towards Stalin on the part of a new generation of young Russians who never directly experienced life under Stalinism, and for whom the gulags are just a distant rumour, even 'fake news'. In their quest for a strong national identity not beholden to the West, they have turned to the icons of the past, not to reclaim or renew their socialist heritage but to reject the savage capitalism that has replaced it.[63] And so the public statues of Lenin and Stalin which were taken down after 1989 and confined to the dark archive of the Communist era (see the cover of this book) are now being taken out of mothballs, dusted down, and given a new lick of whitewash. We see the creation of pseudo-archives of retro-Communist chic, sustaining a politics of false memory in which everything cruel and ugly about the old regime is airbrushed out of the picture of happy smiling masses in an obscene simulacrum of the original *mise en scène*.

I have suggested that these two paradigms of modernity have definite implications for how the historical imagination is exercised around specific events, situations and personalities. A specialised apparatus to legitimise stakes and claims to posthumous public recognition is necessary because in predominantly secular societies organised religion and its priestly caste no longer broker access to immortality for the majority of the population. There is no guarantee that good or bad deeds will secure appropriate residence in heaven or hell.[64] Unless we belong to a faith community, we are left with purely profane strategies for sustaining our posthumous place in the collective memory. This depends not just on the mass media of celebrity culture but on structures of peer recognition. To make a name for yourself increasingly requires mastery of the arts of personal promotion and public impression management; there is now a whole profession dedicated to enabling—practitioners would say 'empowering'—people to succeed in this enterprise. In this context the memoir is no longer an *apologia pro sua vita*, it becomes a hagiographic exercise in do-it-yourself obituary writing based on the principle of *nil nisi bonum*, or 'speak no ill of the dead', leaving behind a eulogised life story which glosses over any disreputable aspects, saying to the reader in effect, 'This is how I would like to be remembered when I am gone'.[65]

If access to posterity has to be negotiated through some process of peer recognition as well as media messaging, there are still two rather different pathways to immortality, which Max Weber was the first to spell out.[66] The first relies on the exercise of charismatic authority, the ritual display of an aura of exceptional capacity (whether of vision or foresight, or some kind of special mastery over events) coupled with the ability to inspire devotion among followers. But how can this authority, so dependent on a metaphysics of presence, continue to be exercised from beyond the grave? That is the special task or avocation of the followers, whose mission is to perpetuate the message of their hero and ensure that it is neither forgotten nor subject to revision in any way. Just as the body is embalmed and all its physical blemishes cosmetically erased, so too all the imperfections of the life are smoothed away in the creation of a seamless master narrative.

I have already suggested that the archive can play a key role in this translation. Not that this necessarily helps to consolidate the posterity. For if grief at the loss of their leader initially brings followers together, the charismatic legacy often sets them at each other's throats, each claiming to be the true heir, the authorised interpreter. Sibling rivalry is not confined to families. Today, in a post-patriarchal society, where filial pieties have given way to those of the affinity group, these conflicts find ever wider relays as charismatics proliferate, in the guise of gurus, mentors and role models, all with their own cult followings, their own interpretive communities, their rival archives of precious words and deeds. The spirit of the dead hero returns by its bad side, in the furies unleashed by this form of ancestor worship.

Weber argued that charismatic authority was inherently unstable and would usually become subject to some kind of 'routinisation', and that is precisely what the archive does. It imposes classificatory order on the more or less chaotic fragments of the exceptional life and gives it authorised meaning, an institutional imprimatur. In Weberian terms, charismatic authority gives way to bureaucratic authority. Peer recognition and reputational identity come to depend on positional, not personal status, the possession of professional competences and accredited expertise guaranteed by a corporate body and disseminated by the archive. Now it is the normative not the exceptional form of historical individuality which is celebrated posthumously. The immortality conferred on the individual by the institution is a primary means of the institution perpetuating itself beyond the life span of its members. Indeed it is a characteristic of the proto-modernist paradigm that it celebrates the 'organisation man' as a mundane principle of continuity linking past and future. In contrast retro-modernism legitimates charismatic authority as providing a quasi-mystical principle of transcendence of the chaotic present, in the figure of a sublime character or genius rising effortlessly above the turbulence of the times to either comprehend or transfigure them, and in the process create a self-perpetuating legacy.

The two strategies of recognition are not mutually exclusive; it is interesting to follow posthumous reputational careers as the dead oscillate between or make the often-painful transition from one status to the other. In fact there is a well-established meta-narrative to ease the move, featuring charismatic rebels mellowing as they age and become establishment figures; again the archive can play a prominent role in securing such retrospective reevaluations. For example, there is the transformation of figures like Nelson Mandela or Che Guevara from antiheroes of armed struggle for the wretched of the earth into icons of a politics of conscience cherished by liberal elites across the Western world. One of the critical tasks of what I am going to call the 'anarchive' is thus to rescue significant figures—for example Paul Robeson, Martin Luther King, Rosa Luxemburg or Emma Goldman—from the enormous condescension and flattery of their posthumous embourgeoisement.

There are also many contexts and conjunctures where individual exceptionalism and positional status merge, for example in the 'cult of personality' where ancestor worship becomes a state religion. Equally, the 'genius' whose work is perceived to transcend the time and place of its creation, and the secular 'saint' who becomes a legend in his or her own life time, both depend on the politics of peer recognition to secure their immortality and, as we say, 'go down in history'. As such they are eminently suitable subjects for archival projects. In contrast, the iconic figures of popular culture, the film stars, rock stars, sports stars, glitterati and public personalities who populate the contemporary hall of fame acquire their aura almost entirely from the dissemination of their activities by corporate and social media. Once their activities are no longer broadcast, they disappear from the public gaze and their fame evaporates. At this point, their own archives and that of their fans may be mobilised to stage a 'comeback' or 'retrospective'. But in most cases this artificial afterlife quickly fades and they become living proof of Adorno's bon mot that organised fame leads to nothingness.

Fame Academies

The landowning aristocracy had no need to become famous. They possessed an inherent and inherited principle of posterity, a patrimony held in trust for future generations. The stewardship of the estate included not only land but also their more or less stately homes in which the fruits of their wealth could be conspicuously displayed: their collections of art and fine furniture, their cabinets of curiosities, their libraries—all these assemblages of cultivated taste were entailed as legacies and required some kind of inventory to be made. In contrast, the new aristocracies thrown up by cultural industries and the knowledge economy in the late twentieth century have a much more tenuous purchase on posterity. Their estates consist primarily of symbolic assets, and for those entrusted with their management the role of the archive is primarily to protect copyright and promote the brand, to authenticate the works and ensure their posthumous dissemination, a project in which financial self-interest and filial observance often happily coincide.

The so-called democratisation of fame, as encapsulated in Andy Warhol's famous adage that 'everyone will be famous for 15 minutes' (more like 15 seconds in the age of Facebook), has disrupted many long-established pathways to immortality associated with social and cultural elites, new and old. It is linked to the space/time compression of the memoryscape and the continual capture, storage and retrieval of transient moments of everyday life in the portable digital archive. The recording of ambient triviality reaches its apotheosis in contemporary celebrity culture with its permanent ephemeralisation of fame as trendiness or fashion.[67]

The notion that everyone can be the star of their own home movie is often said to reflect a culture of narcissism integral to the emotional logic of post-Fordist capitalism: look at me performing the just-in-time production of myself.[68] But I think that this is to underestimate both the complexity of motivation at work and the depth of its entanglement with capital. The drive to capture the epiphanies of everyday life and render them into an inventory of personal significance both mirrors *and* reacts against the state of continual distraction promoted by the fetishism of commodities and the consumer spectacle.[69] The do-it-yourself archive intervenes to transform commonplace mementoes into collectible memorabilia, investing them as objects of attachment with a singular value, a unicity reducible neither to their utility nor, initially at least, to their marketability. But as soon as the archive has rendered these things priceless *and* established their unique provenance they can become fully commodified, usually because of their association with a famous personality or event. In this case the original narcissistic attachment to the object is transferred to the new owner along with its unique aura: buying a pair of Elvis Presley's socks at an auction of the singer's memorabilia may be a way of imagining you are stepping into the King's shoes, but its investment value as a collectible will still depend on its authentication by the Presley Archive.

There are also circumstances in which an archive of creative work, such as the unsold song catalogue of a rock star or the unpublished writing or letters of a famous novelist, can be directly financialised as a heritable asset, either by the artist in their own lifetime or by heirs or legal trustees of their estate. Copyright law can extend future intellectual property rights for up to 120 years after death, so we now have a situation in which guaranteed afterlife far exceeds the lifespan of the artist. Capital, which thrives on transient fashion and the rapid turnover of cultural goods, has nevertheless succeeded in extending its hold on living labour beyond the grave thanks largely to the 'dead labour' embodied in new information and media technologies.[70]

This complicity of the archive with the apparatus of wealth and fame creation poses a profound challenge to its capacity to construct an enduring space and time for the representation of *collective* actions and events. Those social movements which have as their long-term aim the exploration and building of possible worlds other than those created by capitalism find themselves having to rely on their own resources if they want to build an archive to document their endeavours. For many the priority is to devote what resources they have to building the movement here and now rather than documenting its past actions. The environmental movement, for example, is by necessity future oriented and has developed very few platforms for telling its own back story. But does the advent of cyber-space and time change all that?

On Memes and other Mnemonic Devices

As the digital archive penetrates every more deeply into everyday life, as mnemonic memes go viral across the blogosphere, the ever-expanding scale of the information flow is in inverse proportion to the ever more limited scope of its reach. Proto-modernists archive and remember less and less about more and more. Retro-modernists focus ever more grandiosely on minutiae. These foreclosures show how intensely archive fever is fuelled by the de- and re-territorialisation of personal memoryscapes, giving rise to a counter culture of amnesia.

As a general rule, the more accelerated the information flow, the more chaotic its architecture and the more junk space it creates. And the more disorganised the raw material of the past remains, the more archival reason must draw on mnemo-technologies capable of handling large data sets to impose some principle of order on them. Even then, the threat of archival information overload is ever present. There are now so many archives that we see the emergence of organisations, such as the MetaArchive Cooperative, which are intended to facilitate networking among them. This is leading to the creation of a 'dark' archival culture exclusive to those organisations large and powerful enough to partici-pate.[71] As for the rest of us, we all too easily find ourselves back in Borges's famous Library of Babel, 'composed of an indefinite, perhaps infinite number of hexagonal galleries' and populated by those 'who spend their lives searching the shelves and rearranging them, looking for lines of meaning amid leagues of cacophony and incoherence, reading the history of the past and future, collecting our thoughts and collecting the thoughts of others, and every so often glimpsing mirrors, in which we may recog-nise creatures of the information'.[72]

It is worth noting here that the digitalisation of libraries and other collections of paper documents has resulted in what has been called 'tome-cide'.[73] Millions of books have been pulped or otherwise disappeared from the shelves. Some because they are regarded as surplus to requirements; others may not be deemed worth the cost of digitalisation; and most are declared redundant once electronic copies have been made. This culling of a vast repository of printed literature, which is proceeding apace, is based on the assumption that the existence of books qua artefacts is literally a waste of space and that the information they contain can be far more efficiently stored in digital form. The result is to deprive a whole generation of new readers of access to the printed page and to shift the focus of the reading experience from browsing to scanning. At the same time the gain in transparency—no one need get lost any more among the book stacks—has been bought at the price of eliminating the aleatory and serendipitous aspects of archival research. Search engines driven by algorithms may speed up the process of inquiry, but you are much more unlikely to be surprised by what you find.

Borges's prescient metaphor of a global information economy points to a deeper contradiction: the contemporary digital archive can be considered a paradoxical and self-defeating attempt to simulate or re-stabilise customary forms of memory and identity work that its mnemo-technologies have de-stabilised. In fact the archival properties of mnemo-technology have constructed a new form of eventfulness in which the chronological expansion of the present shrinks and produces a widespread sense of its own obsolescence, based on a fragmentary and spatialised sense of concrete duration, captured in instant image/texts.[74]

It is certainly true that digital culture has unsettled the relationship between memory, narrative and the archive. Until recently cognitive science viewed memory as the brain's system for storing, classifying and retrieving information, a storehouse of mental images of the past. In other words, an archive. Equally the archive itself was treated as an external, socialised, and institutionalised form of memory. As long as archives consisted solely of records of one kind or another, and memory was seen as an operation of an individual skin-encapsulated brain, then the equation of the two might have been apposite. But two things happened to upset the metaphoric link. First, cognitive scientists discovered that a lot of memory was autobiographical in form and organised in terms of narrative process. Secondly, digital technologies transformed the way information about the past was coded thanks to the introduction of hypertext links and intelligent search algorithms, so that the archive became less of a *storehouse*, and more of a platform for *storying*—for creating new associations and new meanings from the data in accordance with current needs. Read-only memory and the rigid indexing of traditional archival searches gives way to more dynamic rasters; the overall informational aesthetic of a collection prevails over its classificatory criteria. It begins to look as if *narrative* is now the thread connecting the workings of memory and the archive. So this is a positive gain to set against what is lost in direct hands-on experience through the transition from analog to digital reading.

Nevertheless some professional archivists remain suspicious of the 'smart archive', or at least of its more evangelical advocates. They argue that what really sustains archival research is not the technology but the place itself, the building housing the archive as somewhere a community of scholars can convene, and where the physical encounter with the documentary record occurs. This defence of traditional archival practice has both a progressive and reactionary aspect. The aim is to restore or reinvent the aura of the document as an authentic and unique witness, to retrieve its singular historical value by rescuing it from the all-consuming temporal flux of capitalist modernity, transforming it from a transient trace of mere eventfulness into the reference point for a coherent narrative derived from a close reading of the text itself. At the same time resisting the hollowing out, dispersal or privatisation of collective memory often goes along with shutting out *any* practice that might challenge or erode the archive's privileged hermeneutic role and the ivory tower scholarship it supports.

We have to recognise that despite all the talk of open access and 'democratising the archive', what is happening in many cases is a massive extractive operation in which material volunteered by mainly working-class and minority group informants becomes grist to the academic mill, and helps enlarge the intellectual capital of the professional and creative classes without any compensatory redistribution of knowledge/power. The navigational architecture of many archives, whether digital or analog, often calls for sophisticated research skills and intimidates those who do not have them. For those with dyslexia or other learning difficulties, the problem of access is doubly great.

Whatever conclusion we reach on this point it is in any case premature to argue that we have witnessed an irreversible shift away from the analog to the digital, from memory work embedded in oral tradition and everyday cultural practice to specialised apparatuses which objectify these processes, or to claim that, as far as such a shift has partially occurred, it is invariably negative. It is true that virtual archives tend to generate atomised social networks, and do-it-yourself archiving with digital devices tends to de-historicise and de-politicise the personal memoryscapes. Yet it is also possible to recognise a countervailing movement based on these same digital devices, one which socialises much of the knowledge hitherto confined in official archives and available only to privileged cultural elites. This is undeniably an important step forward. For the fact is that while the proliferation of reminiscence groups and oral-history projects has ensured that the life stories and photographs of more people than ever before have entered the public record, conventional institutional frameworks and even storage locations continue to make such material difficult to access unless you are already in the information loop.

The public credibility—or otherwise—of the traditional archive is explored by the Belgian graphic novelists, François Schuiten and Benoît Peeters in *L'Archiviste*.[75] The narrator-protagonist is a researcher in the department of myths and legends at the Central Institute of Archives in Brussels and is charged with determining whether a number of 'obscure cities', cities which are not on any official map but are the subject of much popular speculation, do in fact exist. He sifts through a mountain of documents trying to determine which accounts are apocryphal or based on hearsay, and which offer genuine proof. He comes to the conclusion that there is sufficient evidence in the form of architectural plans and travellers' tales to support the claim that these cities, in all their immense variety, did exist once upon a time. But this geographical knowledge has been officially suppressed because to acknowledge the presence, even in the past, of these cities would mean that the archive, which represents the collective historical memory, would have to be completely reorganised at great expense to the public purse. Cheaper, then, to destroy the evidence. In order the save the archival project the archivist had to destroy its mnemonic capacity.

L'Archiviste is set in a world where it is still possible for a single archive to encompass and control the collective memory of a society and decide who or what is historically significant and worthy of remembrance. As we have seen, the hall of fame used to be reserved for a pantheon of national heroes, mostly statesmen, war leaders or rich philanthropists, who variously embodied the values of a dominant political class that had no squeamishness about erecting monuments to its own posterity as a way of celebrating, if not eternalising, its economic and cultural power. Yet this is the beginning, not the end of the story.

All those statues of Victorian imperialists which in Britain litter our major city centres were certainly built to last, yet the reputational identities they were meant to sustain have either faded into obscurity or been torn to shreds by revisionist historiography. So should they simply be pulled down and replaced by more relevant figures? The recent campaign

L'Archiviste (Schuiten and Peeters)

by black and other radical students to remove the statue of Cecil Rhodes from the facade of Oriel College, Oxford, suggests that in such cases the all-too-palpable survival of such statuesque figures can serve to focus public attention on the less visible legacy of the values and ideologies they once embodied. In other words they function as mnemonic devices for a counter-narrative, whose themes can indeed become memes.

There is an instructive comparison here with the campaign by the Charlottesville City Council, supported by the University of Virginia, to remove the statute of the Confederate general Robert E. Lee. The violent clash between white supremacists, for whom Lee is an iconic figure, and local antiracists, one of whom was killed, led to a series of highly equivocal and contradictory statements from President Trump, whose sympathies clearly lay with the 'conservationists'. In this case the statue became a rallying point for the alt-right who regarded it as a token of a threatened cultural heritage. With Trump's election they now had the confidence to use it as platform from which to attack 'political correctness'. The danger is that if all such monuments are removed, if only to avoid them becoming the flash points of conflict, it will be too easily assumed that the values of bigotry or chauvinism they embody have also disappeared.

Iconoclasm is ultimately a form of hysterical materialism and magical thinking. As such it is a mirror of iconophilia, the worshipping of images for the sake of their intrinsic power of attraction, which we find in the contemporary art scene, in the work of corporate architects and urban imagineers, driven by the desire to create 'iconic' landmark buildings. But the symbolic power of religion or any ideology is not dismantled by destroying its physical effigies or suppressing its iconography. As we know to our cost these values may continue to flourish underground. Moreover, outside authoritarian states which micromanage every aspect of civil society, no archival institution has a monopoly of the power to define the boundaries of collective memory or control public perceptions of the past.

Technologies of Immortality

Alexander Pope was perhaps the first writer to cast a sardonic eye on the quest for celebrity as a self-defeating existential project: 'What's fame? A fancy'd life in other's breath/A thing beyond us even before our death'.[76] Yet the quest to transcend the all-too-material bounds of human mortality remains as imperative and as impossible as ever. History is by definition a revisionary process and the archive is an integral part of it. Indeed, so

Demonstration to remove the statue of Cecil Rhodes from the facade of Oriel College, Oxford

far from passively preserving the past, archives are the great inventors of tradition. If claims to immortality have never been so contested it is partly because there are now so many rival halls of fame, each of them promoting its own particular brand loyalty, its distinctive archival form, anchored to a specific economy of worth. The moral economy celebrates moral entrepreneurs, the market economy commercial ones; the civic economy bigs up municipal leaders and evangelical bureaucrats, the political economy leading figures from the national political class; the cultural economy establishes the reputation of artists, writers and intellectuals, the knowledge economy that of technocrats and professional experts; and the media economy promotes the icons of popular entertainment, fashion, sport and 'the spectacle'. Of course there are many hybrids: the contemporary glitterati seamlessly connect the worlds of culture, knowledge and entertainment. The obituary columns of newspapers have expanded to accommodate the proliferating media of fame, and so have the numbers and types of archives.[77] Still, this is not a relativistic free-for-all. An overriding power structure persists, ultimately based on the political economy of capitalism, which hierarchises reputational strategies and continues to stratify claims to immortality along lines drawn by class, gender, and 'race'. Death is not yet the great leveller.

The new immortality brokers, distributed across all these spheres, are nothing if not determined lobbyists, variously organised into charities or foundations, professional associations, learned societies, institutes, commemorative committees, fan clubs, political cabals—and archives. Their ostensible aim is to champion the cause of their chosen figureheads and secure for them the best possible posthumous conditions of existence. These are the new priests of a secular belief in life after death, and they practise historiography as a form of faith healing. While it may appear that they are purely altruistic in their devotion to some Great Cause, their investment in their heroes seeks to maximise the rate of return on intellectual, social, cultural or political capital. As we have just seen, those charged with the trusteeship of creative estates have a material as well as a moral interest in promoting their chosen 'brands'.

So where is the Left in all this? To begin with, the present-day Left in Europe and the Americas wants for the most part to dissociate itself actively from all the personality cults linked to the Holy Trinity of Marx, Engels and Lenin (not to mention Stalin and Mao). The pieties of the political catechism or even politically correct thought have no place in 'New Times'.[78] Instead the aim is to create an alternative, counter-hegemonic hall of fame populated with our own heroes and heroines, our own innovators and exceptional individuals who embody our shared values: Trotsky, Lukács, Gramsci or Adorno if you are on the *marxisant* Left; Karl Korsch, Ernst Bloch, Walter Benjamin, Guy Debord, Paul Goodman or Gilles Deleuze if you are on its libertarian wing. Socialist feminists have their own pantheon of Great Women: Louise Michel, the Pankhursts, Emma Goldman, Rosa Luxemburg, Vera Brittain, Simone de Beauvoir, Doris Lessing, Frida Kahlo, and many more. So is the role of the Left archive to collect materials that can stake and substantiate these claims? Will this represent an ingathering of all those who are otherwise marginalised, in death as in life, so as to challenge the existing stratification of immortality?[79] Or is it simply to mirror the fetishism of individual accomplishment at the expense of collective achievement that is such a hallmark of neoliberal capitalism? Or, worse still, to create new articles of faith, new loyalty oaths, new catechisms in place of the old?

When James Agee and Walker Evans 'immortalised' the poor white sharecroppers of the southern United States in their now-classic work *Let Us Now Praise Famous Men*, they set out to document the everyday lives and struggles of people who normally enter history only as faceless statistics of poverty, unemployment and premature mortality.[80] They certainly succeeded in their self-appointed task of giving a human face to the

Great Depression. Yet the success of the book—what made it a classic, and hence perpetuated the lives of the characters it portrayed beyond their mortal span—was the peculiarly intense, poetic and introspective quality of Agee's prose and Evans's photographs. Without that creative testimony, these lives would have gone publicly unrecorded, remaining within the local confines of their family and community memoryscapes; they would not have taken on the aura of emblematic presences in the grand narrative of this epoch of U.S. history.

This leaves us with an uncomfortable question: does it depend on exceptionally talented individuals—in this case a writer and a photographer, but it might just as well be an archivist or an oral historian such as Alessandro Portelli, Svetlana Alexievich or Studs Terkel—to lend poetic substance and enduring meaning to the otherwise unexceptional lives of people whose historical significance is precisely that they bore witness to the impact of larger forces which they could not control, and sometimes did not even fully understand?

At this point we are brought back to what might be called the ethnographer's dilemma.[81] As a condition of providing a space of representation for voices that are otherwise marginalised or silenced, by recording and amplifying what they have to tell to a much wider audience than their peers, in other words by giving them a platform within the bourgeois public realm, the ethnographer serves as an intermediary, or rather an interlocutor, who interprets informants' views to the authorities, and vice versa. Even if the ethnographer consciously adopts the role of advocate rather than neutral 'go-between', even if the interpretive community is widened to include the informants themselves, the actual process of archiving the material collected still usually ensures that it remains within the ownership and control of existing centres for the accumulation of intellectual capital. You have only to look at the Smithsonian in the USA or the Amsterdam Institute for Social History to get the point. So then the question becomes: is there something intrinsic to the archival process that inhibits the redistribution of knowledge power, or is this so only for particular archival forms?

Towards a Theory of Archival Genres

For most of its history in Western culture, the archive has been the exclusive province of the scholar and the bureaucrat, an adjunct to the apparatuses of research, governance and social control. Most of the recent critical debate about the role of the archive has made this assumption. For

Foucault and Derrida, the archive in question is by definition a place where knowledge/power is both concentrated and disseminated by virtue of the legal and bureaucratic documentation it contains, hence its association with the foundations of the state. But while these are still the most important spheres of archiving, they are not the only ones, and in the course of our discussion so far we have come across a number of other types of archives that are gaining in popularity and prestige. Schematically, we may distinguish six general types:

1) The *academic archive*, whose primary purpose is to make an inventory of the sites, sources and content of a discipline's knowledge base, to collect, collate and disseminate research findings, to provide an account of discrete research processes and in general give credibility to the protocols and knowledge claims of scholarship.

2) The *institutional archive*, whose main purpose is to provide a documentary record of administrative and decision-making processes (governmentality), in particular to audit the operations of agencies subject to bureaucratic norms of public accountability and legitimate their claims to effectiveness and/or transparency.

3) The *heritage archive*, whose chief role is to collect images, texts, artefacts and other records related to specific groups or sites considered to be bearers of a particular culture, and to assemble them into narratable formats so that they can be interpreted as a legacy transmissible from one generation to the next.

4) The *conjunctural archive*, whose aim is to construct, preserve and disseminate collective memoryscapes related to a specific event or series of events considered to be of public importance, especially by people directly involved or affected.

5) The *hagiographic archive*, whose task is to document and celebrate the lives of singular individuals or projects, whether alive or dead, famous or otherwise, by preserving and disseminating their work, collecting personal testimonies and other biographical information, and in general promoting or safeguarding their reputational identities.

6) The '*dark archive*': a collection of material which is being preserved for posterity but is deliberately not publicly accessible. Such archives are often online serial publications and databases held by an organisation other than the publisher for future use in case they are lost. Museums, whose main function is conservation, also frequently

contain dark archives—artefacts in their possession which never see the light of day and may not even be properly catalogued. The term has recently been expanded to cover archives generated by the dark web.

Of course these are ideal types, which indicate basic value orientations in the archival mission, and empirically they can be found in any number of weak and strong combinations. There are also specific tensions between these different roles. For example, a heritage archive focussed on a specific event (like the bombing of Hiroshima or Dresden) will privilege the testimony of the victims, whereas an institutional archive like that of the Royal Air Force will inevitably emphasise the individual heroism and sacrifice of the air crews and the conjunctural significance of, say, the Battle of Britain in winning the war against fascism. An academic archive devoted to the Second World War, while it might collect material from both institutional and hagiographic sources would be likely to de-emphasise their heritage aspect and give more space to the conjunctural and contextual dimensions of their significance. The network of archival functions, each having a dark archive counterpart, could be diagrammatically illustrated like this:

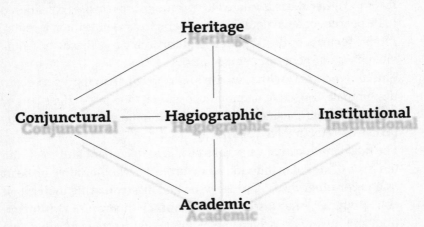

Earlier we distinguished between two basic chrono-topographies, proto- and retro-modernist, but in order to understand how these interpretive frameworks operationalise archival roles, we need to specify the curatorial strategies for accumulating the cultural and intellectual capital which is both invested and realised in building an archive.

There are two possible approaches at work here. The first consists in accumulating *bonding* capital, archival material whose value resides in its capacity to mobilise specific communities of interest and interpretation, strengthen their sense of common identity or purpose and encourage a shared sense of symbolic ownership. The memory work promoted by this archival strategy concentrates on topics that will produce a consensual validation, but by the same token there is a risk of creating an information silo of use to a limited number of users.

The second curatorial approach involves creating *bridging* capital, archival material whose value comes from its capacity to connect disparate fields or groups and establish new kinds of relations between them. Memory work conducted within this frame sets out to build platforms of dialogue around and through the archival collection, opening up new areas of research, acquisition and debate; the challenge here is to avoid amassing so many disparate items that the archive itself loses coherence and becomes impossible to navigate.[82]

We can generate a simple typology combining these variables of chrono-topography and curatorial strategy:

	Proto-modernist	Retro-modernist
Bonding	A	B
Bridging	C	D

How might this work in practice? Let us take the example of an archive dedicated to documenting the 1960s counter culture. A might take the form of a museological project called 'High Art' aimed at fashionistas and collectors of psychedelia, featuring posters, clothes and other design artefacts arranged to demonstrate how they were breaking down the distinction between haute couture and popular culture and challenging the patriarchal traditions of the establishment; B might take the form of a collection of memorabilia associated with a now defunct cult psychedelic band which has retrospectively been seen to prefigure the emergence of punk rock; C might consist of a *catalogue raisonné* of alternative life styles which served as catalysts for new developments in architecture and the arts; D might be a virtual archive containing examples of the influence of new information technologies on counter-cultural initiatives. Or just possibly a museum of underpants worn by guru celebrities in the age of flower power.

In an archive of labour history and working-class culture, A might consist in a historical documentation of rank and file campaigns around workers' rights. *B* might be a collection of cigarette cards featuring foot-ballers, boxers and musicians under the rubric 'A Working Class Hero Is Something to Be'; *C* an archive of press cuttings and interviews about the developing links between miners and LGBT activists during the 1984 strike; and *D* might focus on the influence of organic working-class intel-lectuals on public culture in the interwar years.

So much for function. But what about structure? We have already discussed the different formatting platforms (digital/analog) and their modes of access (open/closed) but to fully grasp the interplay of archival form and content we need to introduce two further mediations which bear directly on the archive's internal knowledge/power relations: its modali-ties of acquisition and its arrangement of material.

In the first instance, we can distinguish between *coded* and *tacit* forms of acquisition.[83] In the first case archival policies follow explicit guide-lines or maxims and obey fixed rules of accession and consignment cor-responding to their declared purpose. In the second archives are more flexible and opportunistic in terms of acquisition strategy, but neverthe-less operate with implicit protocols of what is relevant and appropriate to specific archival needs. As regards the arrangement of material, some archives operate *strong principles of classification and framing*, maintain-ing firm boundaries between different contents, insulating the infor-mation they contain from 'contamination' by other material and tightly regulating the relays via which this information is disseminated. This is how bonding strategies work in accumulating cultural and intellectual capital through the archive, often implemented by *mnemonic missionar-ies* specially charged with the task. Bridging capital, in contrast, requires the relaxation of classification and framing procedures in order to max-imise the scope and scale of interaction between different constituencies of interest. This provides a platform for those we might call *mnemonic entrepreneurs* to get busy.

A more fundamental organising principle which connects archi-val form to content bears on the key distinction made by narratologists between *fabula* and *syuzhet*.[84] An archival narrative of the *fabula* type is organised around relations of temporal and spatial *contiguity*, the chrono-logical sequencing of actions, situations and events, and geographical relations of proximity and distance. The 'story' details successive actions and reactions and relates historical events in terms of the roles played by the main protagonists. Who does what to whom, when and where, under which circumstances and with what outcomes—this is the central narrative issue here. In contrast the *syuzhet*-oriented archive prioritises relations of thematic *contexture* and weaves a chain of associations between different times and places to establish their relational significance. The archive is here dedicated to a particular proposition about how the world works; what drives its mission is usually some ultimate law, moral precept, ideological vision or theory that serves as a higher organising principle for the selection and presentation of material.

Fabula and *syuzhet* are, of course, complementary and not mutually exclusive narrative forms, although as a general rule one is privileged or subsumes the other in any given archival project. In the *populist archive* the aim is to record and celebrate actions, events or situations associated with the heritage and legacy identity of particular groups defined over and against social, cultural and political elites. Such archives often have a mission to articulate and defend a totalising, univocal view of a particular group's place in history, and to underwrite powerful myths of origin and destiny which connect this past to its present and future. Their profile looks like this:

- Capital formation: bonding
- Narrative grammar: *fabula*
- Acquisitions strategy: tacit
- Arrangement strategy: strong classification and interpretive framing of material
- Key actor: mnemonic missionary

A populist archive of the 1960s counter culture would thus concentrate on drawing out the geographical links between different centres of initiative or 'scenes', and the timelines which articulate site-specific conjunctures of activity. A tight line of demarcation would be drawn between the alternative society and the values of the dominant society, but within this frame all manner of material would be assembled, and used to promote a strong positive image and identity for the counter culture.

In mainly but not only academic archives founded on a *hermeneutic* principle, one reflexive statement is systemically related to another via an interrogation of the actions, events or situations they narrate and contextualise. Who knows or does what about what and to whom is the key issue here. Such archives are dedicated to the pursuit of critical knowledge and the overcoming of its obstacles (ignorance, prejudice, etc.) and tend to adopt a pluralistic approach to interpretation. Their profile looks like this:

- Capital formation: bridging
- Narrative grammar: *syuzhet*
- Acquisitions strategy: coded
- Arrangement strategy: weak classification and framing
- Key actor: mnemonic entrepreneur

A counter culture archive organised along these lines would stress the range of political, social and aesthetic initiatives that intersect within the broad rubric of 'the alternative society' and explore their inter-connections, both their synergies and their tensions. The material would be organised thematically rather than in timelines or through a spatial nexus of activity. The interpretive frame would contextualise particular actions, situations and events within a broader reading of the development of advanced capitalist society and its consumer cultures. So curation might concentrate on the conjuncture of psychedelic aesthetics, new information technologies, revolutionary ideologies, and the de-stabilisation of patriarchal codes, unsettling both generational and gender relations, and develop materials around each of these themes.

Each archival type generates its own distinctive mnemonic regime, and creates a field of action around the collection, display and dissemination of its material. The scale of these actors varies enormously, as does the scope of their operation, from individual collectors and do-it-yourself archivists concerned to document a particular individual or event to large corporate and national bodies amassing material to create a grand narrative around matters of widespread public concern.

In the so-called memory wars, archival actors contest and try to invalidate each other's knowledge and relevance claims in relation to a specific historical legacy, inflicting as much reputational damage on their rivals as they can without compromising their own position. Bonders have much more at stake and at risk in these conflicts than bridgers, who may adopt an 'Olympian position' above the fray or simply withdraw from the field altogether. Today memory wars are continually fuelled by identity politics and often revolve around rival interpretations of some iconic figure, canonical text or symptomatic event—and sometimes of all three.[85] It can be very difficult for archives whose raison d'être is to promote a community or ethnic identity to avoid being drawn into these disputes.

A Tale of Two Archives

One of the problems with much of the recent debate is that it has been focused around abstract or normative definitions of what an archive essentially is. Usually it is assumed that its role is primarily governmental or hermeneutic. The argument has got professional archivists quite steamed up, as their practices have come under increasing critical scrutiny, but amid all the deconstruction there has been precious little attention given to what actual archives are like to work in and how they create micro-cultures of meaningful inhabitation for their staff and users. With a few notable exceptions, there is a lack of any ethnographic perspective to provide a thick description of what these sites feel to be in, what explicit and covert messages are conveyed by their spatial arrangements, technical facilities, and administrative protocols and how their public profile is shaped by and in turn influences their physical and social location. What follows is an account of two very different kinds of radical archive, based on field notes made during necessarily brief encounters with staff and users.

The Black Cultural Archive is situated in Brixton, in South London. Once upon a time the area was a major centre of the Afro-Caribbean community presence in the metropolis, a prime place of settlement for the Windrush generation and a front line of confrontation with the police and other agencies of institutionalised racism, culminating in the riots or uprisings of 1981 and 1985. Nowadays the area is subject to intense gentrification, which has displaced many of the long-established residents and turned it into a property hot spot for affluent hipsters and other middle-class professionals, many of them white. Although it has retained its multicultural character, the area's symbolic role as a site of black community has been considerably diluted and it now belongs within a very different cultural geography of race and class.

The development of the Black Cultural Archive (BCA) in many ways reflects these changes. It was originally started by a local community activist, Len Garrison, whose main purpose was to document the everyday struggles and campaigns against racism and discrimination which were either based in Brixton or had a strong presence there. The initial postwar immigrant population coming to Brixton were mainly from Jamaica, whereas Notting Hill, the other main centre of Caribbean settlement in London had people from Trinidad, Barbados and Saint Lucia. One of the early aims of the archive was thus to build links between these different

The Black Cultural Archive

island communities in London, overcoming their historical suspicion and rivalry by stressing the commonalities of black diasporic experience. The focus of Garrison's collection was thus on material related to community campaigns against the 'sus' laws, educational and social discrimination, and the growth of Carnival as an expression of diasporic black culture.[86] He was above all concerned to challenge the dominant representations of black people in Britain, especially the negative stereotypes that prevailed in the media, and to replace them with positive images of black aspiration and achievement. That remains the core agenda of the archive, a bridging strategy connecting the cultural heritages of different communities of African descent but subsumed within a framework of bonding around a common black British identity.

In 2014 the archive moved from crowded premises in Railton Road, on the once-notorious 'front line', to Raleigh Hall, a Grade 2 listed Georgian building which had been derelict for many years and had previously housed a succession of garment manufacturers. In an ironic instance of the Empire striking back, not lost on its staff, the BCA took over a building named after a notorious colonial adventurer from Elizabethan times but now located in the renamed Windrush Square. A good example of how collective memoryscape can be transfigured through urban planning, and the city itself can become a Living Archive of the traces left by communities that settle or pass through it.

With the help of a six-million-pound grant from the Heritage Lottery Fund the building was transformed from its obsolete commercial use into a purpose-built cultural centre, a transition mirroring the process of de-industrialisation which has accompanied gentrification in many parts of London. The exterior of the building is imposing and has been rehabilitated to a high standard, bringing out many of the original architectural features obscured by its long period of dereliction. In addition to the large, temperature controlled, archival space, the building contains a reading room, library, classrooms, an exhibition area, bookshop and cafeteria. The BCA website notes the transition from a small 'amateur' community enterprise to a large professional archive meeting the highest academic standards, with understandable pride, but also with some unease. There are frequent assertions that the archive has remained true to its roots, yet its original community of reference is being rapidly eroded and dispersed through the very processes of urban economic change of which it is itself unavoidably a part.

As a cultural centre BCA is committed to keeping alive the spirit of the Uprisings through its programme of exhibitions and events, as well as extensive archival holdings. The mission is to use heritage as a platform for building links between the ever fewer survivors of the Windrush generation, the Black Power militants of the 1980s and the political anger of today's rappers. Inevitably this leads to a narrative which stresses inter-generational continuities. In the Black Sound exhibition which I visited, the story is organised around a chronological time line, connecting Calypso, R&B, Reggae, Soul, Dub, Drum 'n' Bass, Rap and Grime in a single evolutionary curve powered by black creative energy, embodied in the figure of the DJ, and the struggle for cultural independence associated with pirate radio, indie labels, pop-up music and street culture. *Fabula* trumps *syuzhet* in telling this story: spatial and temporal contiguity provide the main principles of contexture. En route the complexities of black popular culture and its many musics are rather lost: the accommodation as well as resistance to the mainstream music industry, the impact on white working-class youth culture, the generational tensions, the influence and appropriation of and by other cultures and musical idioms, all these wrinkles in the history of Black Sounds are ironed out, leaving a curiously flat impression. Bonding not bridging capital is at work here.

A similar process can be observed in the organisation of the archive. The material is arranged into twelve discrete subject areas or themes (strong classification), each of which is introduced by a short introductory guide, giving a preferred reading (strong interpretive framing), together with information about location and further sources of information. The subject areas chosen reflect the founders' original interests, and include sections on the uprisings, protests and campaigns, the arts, ephemera, publishing, and images of black people in advertising. There are additional sections on slavery, black Georgians, Ansel Wong (a black educationalist), and the black women's movement. The archive is clearly work in progress, but the acquisitions policy seems tacit, despite the explicitly coded agenda of the mission statement. In fact BCA relies on people donating material, it does not have a budget which would allow it to be proactive in seeking to develop its holdings in a long term focussed way. Such an approach inevitably runs the risk of producing a mishmash of disparate materials whose internal connections remain arbitrary or obscure apart from their lowest common denominator, that they are all about the black experience in Britain.

It is partly to guard against possible incoherence that the study guides for each section are so prescriptive. As portals into the holdings they offer clear research guidelines for the reader to follow. For example, in the introduction to the 'Representations' section we read: 'The lack of a positive outlook on black people, cultures and histories in educational textbooks was one of the factors which underpinned much of the education movement in the 1970s and 1980s. The work of organisations and individuals engaged in historical research is important to fight against negative representation. It is important to investigate and promote an alternative history, to give a different viewpoint and to start to unpick racist mythologies and stereotyping'.

Every archive has its own mode of induction to initiate first-time visitors into its mysteries and familiarises them with its peculiar protocols of use. I had emailed BCA a few weeks before my proposed visit but had got no reply. I tried phoning them on the day before to speak to the head archivist, to explain the purpose of my visit and hopefully secure an interview, but there was a fault in their system so that I got caught in a loop and was batted back and forth between two equally unresponsive automated voices. I decided to just turn up and take my chances. When I arrived in the lobby I was greeted by the receptionist, who asked why I had come. I started to explain, but she cut me short and demanded again to know why I was there. After a third 'Why are you here?' I managed to blurt out that I wanted to look at the archive for a book I was writing. 'Why didn't you make an appointment? Everyone has to make an appointment. It says so clearly on the website. Didn't you look at the website? Why didn't you phone in to make an appointment?' I explained about their phone system being out of order. This seemed to mollify her and she checked on her system for my email. She couldn't find it. By now I was beginning to feel a bit like K in Kafka's *The Trial*, caught up in a web of incomprehensible and uncomprehending rules. It flashed across my mind that perhaps I was being given a version of the treatment meted out to the Windrush generation when they first arrived in London. Eventually she decided that I was a bona fide caller, and proffered me two forms to fill in, one stating the purpose of my visit, the other the usual time in–time out register. I was then pointed in the direction of the locker room downstairs, where after a brief struggle with a non-functioning coat rack I eventually managed to cram all my stuff in a locker and make my way into the archive.

At the reading room I was met by a welcoming and informative volunteer archivist. She took me through the online search system, which seemed to work well. One of its strengths is the step-by-step operating instructions and the online connectivity to other archives. Selfishly, I was somewhat miffed to find that the library did not have a copy of *Multi-racist Britain*, a book I edited in the 1990s, but it was explained that they relied on donations and there was no acquisitions budget as such. So although the general parameters of the collection were clearly set out, the actual development and deployment of resources is, of necessity, opportunistic and haphazard. An archive without an acquisitions budget is like an engine with hardly any fuel: it can tick over but not go anywhere.

The reading room was small; it could not have held more than ten people, which I was told was more than enough for average daily usage, mainly by academics and students, so that it was rarely overcrowded. It was a pleasant enough working environment but it could have quickly become cramped. As I had not made an appointment, the professional archivist was not available to bring any documents from the holding area for inspection. This was clearly a post-Fordist delivery model, based on the just-in-time production of material!

On first acquaintance, one of the disconcerting aspects of this site is the mismatch between the rather grandiose aspect of the building's exterior and the intimate interior spaces it houses. The exhibition area, for example, was designed for small displays and it seemed strange that in a building of this size, and with the emphasis on generating cultural activities around the archive, more space was not allocated for this purpose. This scaling down should, in principle, make it easy for visitors to establish little niches where they can feel at home, and certainly once one managed to get past the dragon at the door, there was a relaxed and friendly atmosphere, especially in the cafeteria.

Perhaps the largest constraint on this archive is its commitment to the promotion of positive images. This means it is unable to critically engage with the more problematic aspects of black popular culture, such as the homophobic and sexist stance of gangsta rap, the antisemitism of some Afrocentric missionaries, the presence of Yardies, the relation of street gangs and knife crime to macho codes of black masculinity. The result is to evacuate a space of internal debate *and* leave the field open to Blaxploitation and moral panics orchestrated by the right-wing media. The worst of both worlds.

BCA is keen to stress its difference from conventional, traditional archives because 'it remains rooted in the community that created it'. Yet this is an imagined community in a double sense: it no longer corresponds to the original demographic of Afro-Caribbean settlement, and it represents a one sided view of its contemporary reality. Len Garrison asks 'where are our heroes, martyrs, monuments?' and BCA answers 'all here now, present and correct'. But this question's rhetorical power comes from the more important question it raises: what it would take to no longer need heroes, martyrs and monuments. Yes, a revolution!

BCA clearly has hermeneutic ambitions and its technical architecture is indeed up to the highest academic standards. Yet its rich mix of hagiographic, heritage and conjunctural elements finds common anchorage in an essentially populist message summed up in the strap line which appears on its website: We are One. Ingeniously, but also somewhat disingenuously, the typography composes each letter to give the visual impression of a cubist mosaic. Black identity is allowed to have many facets, as long as it can be recomposed into a single gestalt of meaning.

Arjun Appadurai has argued persuasively that the archive has a distinctive role to play in sustaining diasporic communities through identity building.[87] He notes the tendency to hyper-valorise shared memoryscapes figured by themes of displacement and loss but argues that this needs to be complemented by acts of collective imagination focussed around aspirations for a better future. He writes, 'the diasporic archive must be characterised by the presence of voice, agency and debate, rather than reading, reception and interpellation'. Yet he seriously underestimates the tension, which is often generational, between these twin uses of the archive, as a container of traces of struggles past and as a platform for building intentional community around emergent political demands.

As I walked away from the human warmth of the building into the cold rain and windswept streets of Brixton on a dull grey winter's day, I reflected that perhaps my trip had mirrored the trajectory of the Afro-Caribbean community in Britain, from its initial hostile reception to something like a home from home. This comforting thought was rudely interrupted by being accosted, on the edge of Windrush Square, by a dishevelled rastaman, his locks unkempt and clothes dirty and ragged. He stopped me imperiously with a wave of his wine bottle and demanded some money. He was not pleading, there was nothing ingratiating in his tone, there was no attempt at a sob story, he was asking for an entitlement. Perhaps he staked out the square knowing that visitors to BCA would most likely be fairly affluent middle-class professionals. Unlike the beggars who occupy the porches of Catholic churches, what was being demanded here was not so much alms or an act of charity but the payment of a conscience tax, an act of compensatory justice which redistributed a little wealth from the better off to the poor. I paid up and went on my way.

The incident made me think about my visit. An archive devoted to celebrating the winners, those who succeed in overcoming all the obstacles and making a good life for themselves in what is still a white unpleasant land, runs the risk of turning its back on the losers, whose lives are broken by circumstances not of their own choosing. Treating them purely as victims of a cruel system is to ignore the fact that their lives are just as worthy of recording and of respect as those of the exceptional.

The contrast with Infoshop 56a could not be greater.[88] Located in a back street off the Walworth Road near the Elephant and Castle, one of London's regeneration hot spots, with new blocks of luxury flat now sprouting up to dominate the skyline, the archive is housed at the end of a run-down late Victorian terrace. A scrawled sign directed me to the entrance and I pushed open a battered door festooned with political stickers. I found myself in a narrow hallway, and then pushed into the main archive room where there were two volunteer archivists sitting around

Infoshop 56a

chatting on a couple of scruffy sofas, surrounded from floor to ceiling by open box files, stacked somewhat precariously on wooden shelving. I explained my mission and was ushered into another even smaller room where I was greeted by an impressive white cat and let loose on their material about squatting. By standing on a rather rickety chair I managed to locate some boxes about the Sixties squatting scene, and was immediately transported back half a century to the street commune days. To my delight I discovered some anarchist pamphlets that I had once possessed but lost long ago; unfortunately they were in poor condition, squashed together along with posters and other ephemera in an overcrowded box file.

One of the hidden gems of this archive is its map collection, which largely consists of material produced as part of a local community cartography project and features a wide variety of imaginative hand-drawn maps exploring local people's perceptions of the area and their vision of an alternative future. After about half an hour poring over this material, grateful that I was able to enjoy once again the experience of browsing open shelves, I sat down with one of the volunteers and conducted the interview that follows. As it deals with all the salient points, I have reproduced it in full.

PC: Could you tell me something about the backstory of Infoshop, how did it come to get set up?
VJ: 56a comes out of a broader context of community squatting that was happening in this particular neighbourhood in the 1970s and 1980s, where the whole of Crampton Street was being squatted and there were other, similar streets in South London. People came together after having squatted for a while and having that sense of rootedness in community. They decided they wanted to have somewhere they could meet and eat healthy food, so they set up Fair Shares as a vegan food co-op in 1988, and they still share the building with us. Three years later people who were involved in the anarchist and squatting scene decided to set up the Infoshop. This whole building was squatted up until 2003,when the Council decided to lease it to us, so we have been legal and paying rent ever since.

PC: Is the street still squatted?
VJ: No, none of it is squatted anymore. In fact, as you can see from the surrounding area, encroaching regeneration is all around us, and it's becoming more and more gentrified. Luxury blocks are going up all around us. There is still quite a lot of social housing round here, but in a lot of cases people have bought their flats. Our rent is still reasonably low so we are not about to be priced out of the area anytime soon. The local Labour council here are an aggressively gentrifying outfit, and they are much less supportive of us now than in the early days. It's ironic now we are legal and paying rent, and the Council are our landlords, they are much less sympathetic to what we are trying to do that when we were squatters! Council are now engaged in huge decanting schemes, like the Heygate estate, they have been trying to knock down the Elephant shopping centre, which is the main community hub round here.

When it first started infoshops were quite the thing, they were springing up in lots of places with the idea they were places where radicals could go, if they were travelling or new to an area, somewhere they could go to find out what was happening, where the demos were, what campaign groups to join. Over the years the people involved here built up this huge archive we now have.

PC: So initially you had this immediate community context, where there were a lot of people on the same political wavelength living nearby, but now that contact has dramatically changed. How has this affected how the Infoshop is used and run?

VJ: Things have changed quite a lot. One illustration of that: when we first started we were subsidising the food co-op and now they are subsidising us, in terms of running costs. So nowadays the bike shop and the food co-op are more vibrant and have more of the community about them, and sometimes those people get interested in the archive.

The Infoshop does not have a huge amount of footfall. It's not insignificant, but it's not like it was in the 1980s and '90s. People still come to buy books and zines and sometimes to use the archive. People who use the Infoshop on the whole are the already initiated, those already politically involved, or researchers.

PC: So how did the archive itself get started? Was there any special focus or decision about what would be collected?

VJ: Well, people who come here bring loads of fliers, posters and even pamphlets, so there has never been any shortage of input as regards what you might call ephemera. Obviously the archive reflects the political interests and priorities of the people running it, so we have quite a lot of stuff about the Situationists and about the squatting movement. We have a section of Left publications going back to the late 1960s, mostly British, some American. Then we have stuff that is by category. For example, we have stuff about prisons, police brutality, squatting, stuff from particular regions of the world, boxes on armed struggle, antiracist struggle.

PC: Do you have complete sets of magazines or journals?

VJ: It's a bit random, partly because it quite hard to get hold of some things. In some cases we don't aim for a complete set because that is available elsewhere. For example, you can get a complete set of *Race and Class* at the Institute of Race Relations archive. But they said they were overflowing with stuff so they gave some of it to us where they had duplicates. We have complete sets of our own publications, like *Occupy Times*. And we have copies of *Freedom* going way, way back.[89]

Infoshop 56a

PC: So you have a kind of acquisitions policy, only it's improvised?
VJ: It was much more systematic in the past. It's not as regular as it used to be. Partly this is to do with so much stuff being on the internet. It's a question of whether you go to the trouble of printing stuff out just so you can archive it as hard copy, rather than just archive it online. We have not really got a coherent policy. We still collect stuff from recent events, demos and so on, and of course people bring stuff in.

PC: What about conservation? You have all this material in boxes that over time is going to deteriorate unless you have a purpose-built environment which costs a lot of money you could not afford. Have you thought about digitalising the collection?
VJ: Yes, there has been a desire to move towards digitalisation at some point, but we have not really had the time and resources to do it. The main thing we have had to worry about recently is space. We are fast running

out of space. We have boxes of new stuff needing to be put out so it is accessible, but we have just had to store them. So that means we will have to get rid of some stuff to make room. We have had a policy of having two copies of everything but now we are going to have to get rid of duplicates.

PC: So how do people access and use the archive?
VJ: A lot of people will tweet and email us. We are not the most efficient at that. But it's amazing how many people just drop in. Sometimes we have academic researchers—for example, Alex Vasudevan did a lot of his research for his book on the history of squatting here. It's very informal, people can make themselves a cup of tea ... It may not be what academics are used to, but they get used to it. It's very quiet. We don't have a catalogue as such, and you cannot search the collections online, but it's a fun thing just to root through the material and discover new things. Chris, who started the collections, pretty much knows where everything is, and where to lay his hands on it, but if he is not around, then you have to take potluck.

PC: Are there some sections of the archive that are more used than others?
VJ: The material on squatting and gentrification is probably the most used, which is not surprising, given the local political situation. These are the most updated sections and where we still have some semblance of a link between this space and political activism. In the 1990s this space was much more vibrant in terms of links to movements like Reclaim the Streets or the squatting movement, but now there is not that clear link. There are other spaces, not archives as such but centres in other parts of London, which are more directly connected to political activism. The emergence of Momentum has drawn a lot of people into Labour Party stuff, which is not irrelevant but not our thing, and they wouldn't hang out here.

PC: How do you envisage the future of Infoshop. Will you be creating a catalogue to make stuff more accessible?
VJ: There was a move at one point to make a catalogue, but not online. It was more for our own use so we could find our way around. We are all volunteers. None of us are professional archivists or trained librarians! The zine archive is more catalogued than the rest. But things change here very slowly. In a way that's the nice thing, to have one place in London where things don't change very fast.

PC: Well, I suppose one of the roles of an archive is to provide a safe haven for stuff that might otherwise be lost or just be swept away by the tide of history.

VJ: That's it, and that's one way we are a little bit different from some of the newer radical social centres. For example, there has been a place in Bethnal Green called Common House. It's a great space used by lots of groups—reading groups, meetings, stuff like that—but they are paying private rents which are very high and are already in financial trouble. D-I-Y Space, which is a kind of gig/performance space, are also having difficulties. We are still the only independent, self-funding, self-organised archive for radical political culture in London. We are not dependent on grants from external bodies. So these places are very precarious, whereas Infoshop is more sustainable. We have a fifteen-year lease at a relatively low fixed rent.

PC: What about activities around the archive?

VJ: Well, as you can see, there is not much space but we have had meetings and workshops here; for example, a prison letter-writing group meets here. We have had some important reading groups meeting here.

Generally it's been low in capacity and energy in the last few years. Sometimes it feels as if we are just hanging on. Obviously it's run by volunteers and it depends on how much time they can spare. All of us are busy with other things. We do fundraisers now and then, but recently there's not been much proactive energy to take on new archival projects. We would like it be more a bookshop than it is at present, but getting a new book order together is quite a big deal for us.

Unlike a lot of the newer spaces, we have an open-door policy: you don't have to make an appointment, you don't have to form a user group, you can just turn up.

A lot of like-minded people from abroad come here to check out what's happening in the anarchist scene in the UK. There are still regular squatters' nights when people can come and get information, legal advice and so on, even if squatting is extremely hard at the moment. A lot of people like to hang out here. We get quite a lot of people who hang out here who are quite socially isolated, quite lonely.

PC: Do you have any sense of the archive as containing a political heritage or legacy to hand on to a younger generation? Do you have young

people coming here? Do you have links to schools and colleges in the areas?

VJ: Yeah, we would like to do more educational work. We had someone contact us recently who works with seventeen-year-olds, teaching them advocacy skills. She brought a group of about forty kids to the archive and asked me to give them a short talk explaining what we do here and what anarchism is. It was great, they were really interested and they were local, from Brixton and the Elephant and Castle. We also have students from the College of Communications who come here and do projects.

Infoshop 56a could easily be written off as a good (or bad) example of anarchistic principles of organisation. For those brought up on the bureaucratic protocols of the academic or governmental archive, the absence of any stable system of classification or cataloguing, a haphazard acquisitions policy and general ramshackle structure disqualifies Infoshop from being regarded as a functional archive at all. Yet there is a method in this madness, as the volunteer makes clear. In this case weak (or rather nonexistent) interpretive framing is tempered by stronger thematic classification. Nevertheless anyone visiting the collection who did not have a basic mental map of the Libertarian Left would be likely to feel bewildered by the sheer variety and range of material on display. This sense of disorientation is not helped by the cramped conditions; there are no desks where stuff can be properly laid out and perused.

The interview gives us a very clear picture of how important physical location and community of reference is in shaping the development of an archive. In a rather different fashion from the Black Cultural Archive, gentrification and the dispersal of its original demographic have dislocated the Infoshop from its social and political base. There is a pervasive tone of melancholy in the account, a sense of being stranded by the tide of history, the front lines of struggle having moved on elsewhere. Yet this is tempered by the sturdy notion, which Walter Benjamin would have approved, that the issue may not be about how to accelerate the pace of technological change but of interrupting it and that one of the revolutionary functions of the archive is to create spaces of deceleration, to 'stop the runaway train of history'.[90]

If the infoshop model is to survive, it will need more than low maintenance costs to ensure its sustainability. It will have to evolve from being the vehicle of a political subculture, an asset only available to the already initiated, into an open-access platform of political education aimed at 'Generation rent'. In other words it has to shift from bonding to bridging in its approach to capacity building. Unfortunately its commitment to a rather purist form of anarchism prevents it from reaching out to Momentum and the Corbyn-led Labour Party, and this larger political isolation has its own is local demographic correlate. Infoshop's Green credentials may be impeccable but while veganism and cycling may go down well with New Age hipsters, they are unlikely to appeal to the local BAME community, let alone what is left of the South London white working class.

It is interesting to compare Infoshop with the MayDay Rooms (MDR), since they have a very similar agenda in terms of documenting the Libertarian Left since the 1960s in Britain. But the similarity ends there. MDR occupies a prime site in Fleet Street, strategically located opposite the London head office of Goldman Sachs and was established in 2006 with a large grant from the Glasshouse Trust, the personal foundation of a member of the Sainsbury family who is a well-known patron of the artistic and political avant-garde.

The building is on five floors plus a roof garden, with spacious rooms and state of the art digital technology. It is home to a number of radical publications and campaigning organisations, but at present its holdings are nowhere near as extensive as Infoshop. Its collections mainly span the period from the late 1960s to the mid-1990s. There are a few large holdings (Statewatch and Greenham Common), but most are modest in size and cover themes ranging from counter-educational initiatives (A-Course, Schooling & Culture, the Anti-University) to social protest (Poll Tax Rebellion, Jubilee 2000 Afrika Campaign) and counter culture (Scratch Orchestra, Queeruption). Other material gathered relates to collective publishing endeavours and activist collectives such as Wages for Housework and Big Flame. Supplementing these areas, MDR has a growing collection of pamphlets, flyers, and other ephemera—from pamphlets to journals and flyers. Despite its explicitly coded policy of forging links between past and present struggles, the archive lacks organic links with working-class and BAME communities struggling against gentrification and social cleansing in London. Its symbolic location at what was once was the heart of the newspaper industry paradoxically marginalises it within this more salient political geography.

The reader will by now have realised that for autobiographical reasons my sympathies lie with Infoshop. Despite, or rather because of its scruffiness, it felt more like an archival home, somewhere I could imagine spending time and doing research. But my head tells me that the future belongs to archives that can adapt digital information technology to the task of creating new platforms of civic engagement, especially where these are linked to the renewal of community on the front lines and backyards of capital's war against living labour. It is to the terms of that challenge that we must now turn.

Between *Realpolitik* and *Dingpolitik*: The Living Archive in a 'Post-information' Age

Typologies may be useful in helping us understand the limits and conditions of different archival strategies, the constraints on possibility, as well as the advantages of particular ways of defining, selecting, acquiring, organising, interpreting and disseminating archival material. But such a reading of archival genres, while it may be of interest to archivists themselves, must, if it is to have any wider bearing, be supplemented by an understanding of their role in the political ecology of the information society.

If there is an alternative to the proto- and retro-modernist paradigms of remembrance, it might come from reconsidering history-as-legacy, not as a way of immortalising the past, or amortising our debt to it, but precisely in order to 're-mortalise' and revalue it. And this bears directly on an existential reality I touched upon at the beginning, albeit more from the point of view of the archivist than the archivee. When we die, our most intimate possessions and the stories bound up with them are scattered by the winds of change, sometimes to the four corners of the globe. In tracing this diaspora of things we can actually reconstitute the trajectory of a life, its social networks and the extent and limitations of its reach. Yet this is only the beginning of the story. Our precious things, the things which evoke for us important moments or people in our lives, may be fragile, and need to be cherished, but unless they are tokens of the relationship we actually had with those on whom we bestow them, they cannot retain their original significance. Objects, I have argued, are promiscuous, bestowing their meaning on whoever adopts them and treats them well. That is their *realpolitik*. So these remains always elicit a re-minding in another sense, because, once re-told, re-evaluated, re-concentrated in a different narrative, they begin to function in a memoryscape different from their donor's; it is only on condition that they do so that they survive as part of a Living Archive, a history of the present. This revisionary principle holds true even when an archive is specifically dedicated to the task of perpetuating someone's memory. This perpetual revisionism is the defining characteristic—the '*dingpolitik*' of the Living Archive, and one of the conditions under which its contents perdure.

Revisionism has been something of a dirty word within the Left and Labour heritage industry, which is dedicated to finding a 'useful' past—one that has legacy lessons for present struggles. Any attempt to deconstruct these invented traditions of militancy or challenge a utilitarian stance towards history tends to get lumped together with ideologically hostile projects aiming to undermine core values and achievements of popular democratic struggle. Typically this heritage work, addressed primarily to the working-class or minority ethnic communities whose stories it tells, is driven by a desire to overcome the cultural discontinuity and social dislocation they have experienced as a result of globalisation, especially through the processes of deindustrialisation or mass migration. The curatorial aim is to re-connect past, present and future into a single seamless narrative of struggle and hence restore broken links between the generations.

This is a laudable ambition but all too often it produces tunnel visions allowing little or no room for the contingencies and contradictions, the historical *singularities* that make these stories both interesting and unrepeatable. Especially where the focus is on activist life histories, and on their promotion as positive role models for the young, the temptation is to read everything that took place in the subject's childhood and youth retrospectively as leading up to the moment of commitment to the Cause: a secular version of the religious conversion story. Of course activists are not born, they are made by the circumstances they fight against, but in so many of these accounts fate, destiny or chance (being in the right place at the right time) become self-fulfilling principles of explanation. Militancy becomes a cause of itself as an effect. In the terms I have proposed such archival projects are proto-modernist in orientation, privilege bonding over bridging capital in their development, and operate tacit but strong classification and framing rules in arranging and interpreting material. They rely on and encourage mnemonic missionaries.

In contrast, the Living Archive needs to link biography and history as an exercise in sociological imagination (after C. Wright Mills) through the application of *multiple* perspectives, gearing through different scales and scopes of intersection, from the most concrete to the most abstract and without reducing one to the 'expression' of the other, i.e. individual agents seen as being driven by social forces, or, conversely, history consisting of a chain of events whose prime mover is individual agency or will power.[91]

In fact, contra Marx, the very notion of individuality—of a human subject always and already identical to its own thoughts or actions—is decentred by history, which inserts a principle of counter-finality, of uncertainty and unintended consequence, between any given project and its outcome. The map of a life, however clearly drawn, is always both more and less than its territory. The Living Archive should be about opening up that potential space of *under*-determination.

By the same token the political agency that 'makes history' becomes radically eccentric to itself in so far as its programmatic intentions find their only centre of articulation in the processes it helps to set in motion but which by definition exceed its grasp. Manifestos have only tried to change the world; the task for the Living Archivist is to interpret them, to provide the resources which will help us decide if they are genuinely performative or merely acts of wish fulfilment.

The Adoptive Archive: A Thought Experiment

An archive of any kind implies a theory or map of the terrain it covers. For a concrete sense of what this entails, let us briefly return to the project of an adoption archive. The Living Archivist has to map and make sense of the whole terrain of adoption history in a way that remains rooted in the experience of adoptees but also embraces the stories of birth parents, adoptive parents, social workers and other professionals, all of whom are parties to the adoption contract, willingly or not. The archive has to create a space of representation in which these different standpoints can be registered and enter into dialogue, confrontation and debate. It also has to encourage users to identify lacunae, add fresh evidence, and pose new questions. Equally, this conversational space has to be more than an ongoing mash-up of information. It has to be *organised*, structured thematically so as to contextualise the field of adoption studies around the issues of class, race, gender and sexual orientation intrinsic to it.

For example, here are some possible themes that connect the making and contesting of adoptive identities to a wider set of debates about the family, citizenship, state intervention, and the boundaries of national and racial identity.

a) *Naturalisation*: notions of bonding, natural parenthood, and natural rights; the naturalisation of adoptive identities and the naturalisation of 'aliens' by the state.

b) *Assimilation*: the analogies and substantive links between adoption into another family and assimilation into another culture; the infantilisation of the immigrant and the acculturation of the adoptive child; dual consciousness and building a home from home; practices of 'passing'.

c) *Body Politics*: imagined kinship and community; the boundaries of identity and the frontiers of belonging.

d) *In the Name of the Law*: the legalisation of identity and illicit existences; passports and papers as sources of legitimation and anxiety; the name of the father in the adoption story and the mother tongue in myths of ethnic origin; baby farming and forced separation of adoptees from their mothers.

e) *Mirror Stages*: the practice of 'matching' in adoption and in the screening of immigrants; positive images and religions of identity; mimicry, stereotypes, and the subversion of imposed roles in adoptive families.

f) *The Hidden Curriculum Vitae*: the role of cover stories in denying difference; censorship and disclosure; the body image as a container of what is hidden from case histories; underground memories; the past as foreign country.

g) *Teleological Tales*: rags to riches and other success stories; atrocity stories and victimologies; tales of redemption, child rescue and the civilising mission; adoption and the family romance.

h) *The Quest for Origins*: separation, displacement and loss; the anxiety of influence and the search for an authentic self; the quest for roots and the desire to know.

The key question then would seem to be whether such themes (or others) emerge spontaneously from the material itself or are imposed either a priori or retrospectively. Yet to set the issue up this way rests on a false premise. Patterns of meaning never emerge spontaneously from material but are produced through a reading process that always involves implicit strategies of interpretation. For example, the populist adoption archive, as we have just seen, would favour a mash-up strategy, bringing together quite disparate sources: policy documents, case histories, memoirs. In contrast the hermeneutic approach produces clearly demarcated lines of enquiry. Yet the adoption story cannot be scripted either by relying solely on oral testimony or by feeding it into some kind of 'theory machine' and cranking the handle so that everything falls into its preordained narrative place. It is in the interplay between sources of information and sites of dialogue, between the *dingpolitik* and the *realpolitik* of its operation, that the archive comes alive.

The Adoption Archive necessarily introduces a principle of discontinuity as a *link* between past, present and future lives; it brings into focus the more-or-less violent discordances which events can create in the lives of those caught up in them. So adoptees' life stories tend to either hinge on the split between 'before' and 'after' the moment of adoption or revolve endlessly around the moment of abandonment—a moment too traumatic to be fully articulated or integrated. The temptation, then, is to make these stories bear inert witness to the quest for some therapeutic 'closure'. The pressure is to avoid opening up old wounds and to underwrite the meta-narrative that bad beginnings can lead to happy endings. The temptation should be resisted. What is required is to provide some narrative scaffolding to serve as a prop or prompt enabling painful or repressed experiences to be put into words.

Left Field and the Quest for Uncommon Ground

This example reminds us that the true task of the Living Left Archive is to serve as a navigational device between an otherwise occluded past, an impassable present, and an unthinkable future, reconnecting these frozen time signatures within a dialectics of concrete duration. This demands an alternative notion of the exceptional, to remove it once and for all from the seductive grasp of individualism without falling back into a hypostasised notion of collectivity. We need to retrieve and depict the genealogy of actions, events or situations considered exceptional not in terms of personal heroics but inasmuch as they depart from existing norms and challenge the dominant consensus or common sense. Individual stories have to be placed within the trajectory of the events or situations they are caught up in *without* reducing their meaning to this generative context. Marx's notion of historical individuality, which identifies transformative individuals and groups solely on the basis of their relation to the class struggle, is a crudely reductive attempt to connect biography with history. Yet, by the simple device of substituting gender, sexuality, or 'race' for class, it has continued to inform many archival projects associated with progressive identity politics. Instead we should pursue the notion of singularity as it has been developed by complexity theory, in which the intersection of biographical and historical contingency is treated as a *manifold* whose relays of meaning are subject to sudden and unpredictable change.[92]

There is an added factor to exceptionalism in the case of the Left Archive. Confronted with the brute facts of injustice, pitted against indifferent or afflicted powers, subject to the catastrophes of second nature, ordinary people do the most extraordinary things. They perform exceptional feats of endurance, acts of generosity or self-sacrifice, and labours of love and mutual aid that in more ordinary circumstances they would not be imagined capable of, least of all by themselves. No one who has been privileged to witness this glimpse of true human possibilities can ever forget it. At a time when everything that is solid about such solidarities seems to have melted into air, it is worth remembering, documenting and celebrating such moments when a real culture of fellowship emerges in what David Graeber has rather mischievously called 'actually existing communism'.[93] Whether it is the Stephen Lawrence Campaign or Justice for Hillsborough, or Black Lives Matter, not to mention countless other, smaller and less well publicised campaigns, each has its own distinctive discourse, its site-specific idioms of political engagement, its characteristic jokes, stories, slogans and songs, its passionate internal debates, its rituals of affiliation. As Graeber points out, we have hardly begun to create an ethnography of such movements. A lot of the Left dismisses them as 'single-issue' campaigns, ignoring the new affinities and alliances that are created, the often translocal networks of association that spring to life. But it is precisely here that prefigurative forms of a more inclusive and participatory democratic politics can be found.

This is not to say that we should exempt such instances of collective action from critical scrutiny. The emotional and ideological bonds formed during struggles can all too easily become double binds, and friendships can also foster enmities. The culture of activism imposes its own limitations. As anyone who has spent time in one of the sectarian *groupuscules* of the far Left can testify, the stereotype of the political activist as a humourless ranter who lives only for the next 'demo' and is never happier than when taking to real or imagined barricades is not an entirely fictional character. At any rate, to counter this stereotype we need 'warts-and-all' accounts, not sanitised or sentimentalised—let alone sensationalised— versions of events. Only then can we make a deep mapping be made of

the shifting networks of affiliation and influence connecting and discon-
necting the manifold configurations that make up the field of Left political
culture.

Equally important, the Living Left Archive has to address the blind
spots in its own preferred readings, not just the moments or movements
consigned to the footnotes in the authorised accounts but the micro-poli-
tics of everyday life that do not register on the leftist radar because they do
not adopt the kind of rhetorics, campaigning strategies or organisational
forms that are recognised as part of the repertoire of 'doing politics'. So
in addition to scavenging in the dustbins of official Left historiography, it
is important to actively seek out emergent groups and new practices. For
instance, small acts of guerrilla gardening and do-it-yourself urbanism
are as worthy of documentation as the big actions of the Occupy movement from which they often draw inspiration. Scaling down is as important as scoping up when it comes to assessing the archival significance and
legacy value of particular actions.

If we had to identify where the kind of archive I am talking about
belongs within a wider political and cultural geography, I think that we
might call it 'Left Field'. Derived from baseball, the phrase "out of left field"
may have originated because the left fielder has the farthest throw to
first base—a difficult throw to execute and, being so unexpected, likely to
disconcert the batter trying to reach first base. The term migrated into
general use in American vernacular, referring to anything unexpected
or out of the ordinary, and this element of surprise may have positive or
negative connotations. So it could mean odd, perverse, weird or outright
crazy, out of touch with reality; but it could also mean unconventional,
innovative, groundbreaking, transforming reality. With the advent of
the Hippies, Left Field became synonymous with 'far out' or 'way out', a
point of departure or self-distancing from the dominant reality principles of 'straight' (bourgeois/capitalist) society, usually as part of a wider
quest for some alternative 'higher' state of being. From here it was but a
step to render it into a metaphor for the subversive/disruptive end of the
political spectrum and for the term to become associated with revolutionary Left represented at this conjuncture by the Weathermen and Black
Panthers.

The term was not much used in Britain and certainly not by the more
inward-looking sections of the British Left who remained deeply suspicious of all things American, except possibly jazz and noir movies, until

the advent of postmodernism when it got taken up by the arts establishment, curators, gallerists and critics, who used it to promote the originality of artists whose work was not otherwise on the cultural map. In this context the term took on the connotation of 'something coming suddenly out of nowhere', though a singular act of creative inspiration. Uncoupled from the ideology of romantic individualism, Left Field might also point towards the *uncommon* ground from which counter-hegemonic movements emerge and which they in turn help to create. It is where all questions become mootable, and where the most unlikely things are brought together and assembled for consideration or debate. It is that ground which the Living Left Archive must seek to occupy.

Lest We Remember, Lest We Forget: On Iconoclasm and the Problematics of Silence

We can only forget what we have first remembered. I have suggested that it is sometimes necessary to let the past go, but remembering to forget is always going to be more difficult than forgetting to remember. Collective remembrance atrophies unless it is enacted in specific social occasions and organised through ritual events. The commemoration of war is a good case in point.

The experience of war, by both military and civilian populations, is one of those instances where involuntary and private memories are necessarily linked to a public and officially sanctioned narrative in ways that still may be open to challenge. War cemeteries, museums and monuments may be the most visible sites of commemoration, but there are also national oral-history archives and a host of smaller, more local ones which arrange similar events.[94] Whether triumphalist or revanchist, whether they celebrate the sacrifice of those who died for a Great Cause or simply mourn the loss of human life, these archives are dedicated to the task of keeping the meaning of war alive for generations who have grown up in peacetime and have no direct experience of the horror and suffering war brings. 'Lest We Forget' is the cautionary banner under which most of these projects assemble their material, but this does not always guarantee a pacifist message. Indeed the way some go about honouring the dead may pose problems for those who abhor militarism and warmongering and regard recent interventions in Iraq and Afghanistan as simply the continuation of imperial wars that killed nearly a billion people in the twentieth century.

plore this issue I carried out a small online survey looking at activists and academics of various affiliations were responding pate of public commemoration around the centenary of the start of rst World War.[95] I emailed a short questionnaire, in the first instance ny personal network of friends and colleagues, with the request that ley should pass it on to their own social and professional circles. Quite quickly I had a largish sample, broadly based in terms of age and viewpoint, drawn not only from academics (although they were the largest group) but also from people working in the cultural industries or in public-service and community organisations. The majority were highly critical of the revisionist message being relayed through much of the media—namely that the war was a futile and tragic enterprise redeemed by the heroism and fortitude of the common soldier. They felt, quite rightly in my view, that this evaded a lot of important political issues. So far, so predictable. But what surprised me was that the vast majority did not know about or just ignored the traditional two minutes of silence on 11 November. I asked what people thought about during this time, only to discover that most had simply carried on with business as usual. A few consciously boycotted the event either as an anti-militaristic gesture or because they were fed up with the saturation media coverage. The few who did observe the silence all had personal memories of members of their family having been in one of the world wars, in many cases being killed or injured. The existence of such a large unsilent majority gave me pause. In the light of answers to some of the other questions, it seems likely that what was involved here was an act of dissociation from official one-nation memory politics and its links with popular patriotism.

Taken as a whole, the responses were singularly unmindful of the deep resonance of the event and its aftermath for large sections of the population, including those from the ex-colonies whose grandparents had fought and died in it. Because the First World War did not feature as significant in their personal memoryscape it was regarded as politically irrelevant. In this respect the unsilent were endorsing the very social amnesia that in other contexts they would be the first to condemn, while isolating themselves from many people whose hearts and minds they are seeking to influence. If only they had used the two minutes of silence to reflect on that!

This little exercise raises a number of important issues that David Rieff has recently addressed in his essay 'In Praise of Forgetting'.[96] Drawing on his experience as an observer and commentator on recent wars in Iraq, Lebanon, Bosnia, and Ireland—wars in which external military intervention only exacerbated the existing civil, ethnic and religious conflicts— Rieff questions the widespread moral imperative to create archives and monuments around them. Such projects, he argues, may be a way of continuing the war by other means, since all parties, the losers as well as the winners, seek to collect evidence to support the justice of their cause. Indeed, those who lose the war sometimes win the peace in that their account of the conflict's meaning prevails in retrospect. Certainly, then, there may be circumstances in which peace and reconciliation are best served by forgetting, by refusing to dwell on the past and rake over the embers of conflicts which, if not fully resolved, have at least reached a provisional settlement.

In some instances, where open antagonisms are the bitter fruit of enduring and deep-rooted divisions within civil society, the situation is even more complicated and fraught. Should we be building archives around the 'race wars', or the 'culture wars' that broke out in the 1980s around the identity politics of gender and sexuality? Would this be about investigating a space of retrospective reconciliation between conflicting positions, or simply keeping the flames of anger alive so that a new generation may relight the torch? And what about the 'class war' which has been widely declared over by both the winners and the losers in post-industrial societies, even if it continues through other more 'diplomatic' means in insidious forms of symbolic violence that inflict hidden wounds?[97] In a UK context, do we consign events such as the Poll Tax Riots or the Miners' Strike of 1984 to the Museum of Labour History and move on, concentrating on documenting new and emergent sites of popular democratic struggle such as the environment and global warming? Or do we insist, under the banner of 'Lest We Forget', that the long history of these struggles still needs to be embedded in some kind of class discourse, however updated, in order to make sense of (and to) the twenty-first-century precariat?[98]

While ensuring that archives do not artificially prolong struggles that really are anachronistic, we also need to make sure that they do not become substitutes for the development of new campaigns, drawing in energies and resources that would be better expended on contemporary issues. Is it really worth spending a lot of time and energy on researching the Greater London Council archives in order to recreate the glory days of 'Red Ken' Livingstone and his administration when there is so much that

done right now to combat the stranglehold which neoliberal
..as over the governance of London, not to mention the need to
. municipal socialism beyond the state-sponsored populism which
.cterised that era of Left politics?[99]

How then to reconcile the claims of the past, the desire to remem-
.r, with the demands of the future and the will to forget? Given the frac-
.ured chrono-topographies I have outlined, there are clearly no readymade answers. At the very least, we have to recognise that contemporary
archive fever is partly a necessary response to a profound if selective
cultural amnesia fuelled by the planned obsolescence of Instagrammatic
memory work. In a sort of reverse Alzheimer's, short-term memories
crowd out long-term ones and threaten to make the re-historicising function of the archive redundant. In fact short-termism and the quick-fix
culture is becoming a general characteristic of both emotional *and* economic investment strategies under late capitalism, a response to the vola-
tility of markets *and* the chronic instability of the life course. Why plan
ahead when the future is so uncertain? Why remember what is always
and already out of date?

Short-termism can also have direct consequences for the sustainability of the archive itself. One recent example was the decision by the senior
management of Ruskin College, Oxford, to destroy its archive of student
records going back to its foundation in 1899 as the flagship of independent
working-class education. Labour historians, educationalists and many
others protested than this was an act of pure vandalism, erasing the collective experience of generations of working-class students and destroying an important source for the study of a movement that also embraced
Working Men's Colleges, Miners' Libraries and other institutions that
nurtured the formation of an organic working-class intelligentsia. The
rationale for the decision was simply that the College no longer had the
space or the resources to house this archive or to make electronic copies
of the documents, but behind this was a sense that these records had no
historical value. And behind *that* was a disavowed desire to 'modernise'
and 'reinvent' the college by distancing itself, as Blairite New Labour had
already done, from its links to the labour movement.

One interesting project which re-establishes a properly *dialectical*
relation between remembrance and forgetting can be found in the work
of the conceptual artists Esther Shalev-Gerz and Jochen Gerz, in particular their Monument against Fascism. The work was commissioned

Monument against Fascism, Hamburg

by the municipal authorities in Hamburg in the early 1980s against the background of a rise in popular support for the Neofascist Right. It took the form of a 12-metre-tall, lead-clad square column situated in a bustling working-class neighbourhood. The artists appended the following announcement to the work:

> We invite the citizens of Hamburg, and visitors to the town, to add their names here next to ours. In doing so we commit ourselves to remain vigilant. As more and more names cover this 12-metre-tall column, it will gradually be lowered into the ground. One day it will have disappeared completely, and the site of the Harburg Monument against Fascism will be empty. In the end it is only we ourselves who can stand up against injustice.

Between its inauguration on 10 October 1986 and its disappearance on 10 November 1993, the monument was progressively lowered into the ground several times, and some seventy thousand signatories inscribed their names on it. So where the column once stood there is now an underground archive containing the names of all those who by their signing made an act of commitment to continue the fight against fascism so that no more monuments like this would be needed. Its disappearance was thus paradoxically the antithesis of the erasure of Germany's Nazi history by

the Holocaust deniers of the Far Right. It also departs from the lurid commemoration in spectacular monuments which encourages dark tourism.
Instead, their 'anti-monument' provides spectral evidence of the need to
continue the struggle in order precisely to move on from the past while
still remembering not to forget it.

A Living Archive is one that is aware of its own inevitable transience and that one day it may be no longer need to exist. Archival projects
dedicated to the proposition that history proceeds by its bad side should
actively work for their own extinction in the same way as the Monument
against Fascism. Beware the archive of atrocities that has as its main (if
disavowed) purpose its indefinite perpetuation! In fact an archive is only
alive if it deals with death by facilitating the work of mourning, enabling
survivors to let go of the past, but it can only do that if it sustains an open
framework with the capacity for new information and interpretation to
be added all the time, creating an ever-changing palimpsest.

Archival In/Disciplines

The aim of the Living Archive must be to provide a platform for the living
labour of research, sustaining curiosity and the desire-to-know as against
any form of academic scholasticism; mnemonic technology has to be har-
nessed to *this* task rather than circulating the dead labour of past generations of scholars. But if it is to do this, it has to break with the dominant
culture of research based on the 'hands round the text' reading model in
which academics work in splendid isolation to produce learned mono-
graphs for consumption and, hopefully, approbation by their peers. At
the very least this must mean challenging the disciplinary boundaries
drawn by the academic division of labour in favour of a trans-disciplinary
approach to archiving.

The issue is not confined to the humanities and social sciences. It is
the great failure of traditional Left political culture to have produced a
one-dimensional view of what the political process is about, a view that
may eschew the narrow electoral preoccupations of the established political class but nevertheless mirrors its reduction of *bios politikos* either to
participation in a disembodied, bureaucratised system of governance
or to its negation in mass mobilisations and popular assemblies. But
there is more to politics than voting or rioting. As Foucault showed us,
the administration of things always involves the disciplining of bodies,
and as Raoul Vaneigem and Roberto Unger have insisted from their very

different perspectives, the re-enchantment of the civic realm as a stage for the enactment of direct democracy always requires rediscovering the passionate and the ludic, the mythological and the ritualised as distinctive biopolitical idioms.[100]

Genuinely to enlarge the imaginative reach of collective memory, the Living Archive must register these more subtle dimensions of political agency and voice in—and sometimes against—the crude thinking of political rhetoric. To this end it has to become more deeply embedded in everyday networks of communication, whether virtual or face-to-face, that sustain conversations about matters of shared concern whether they occur in the street, the supermarket or the shopping arcade, the workplace or the 'leisure centre'.

This kind of agenda requires not just a formal commitment to transdisciplinarity but a substantive *methodology* that can actually deliver it.[101] In terms of the conceptual vocabulary I have proposed, this means weak classification of already coded knowledge plus strong framing of its emergent and tacit interpretive properties as a means of accumulating bridging capital.

Actor-network theory (ANT), as developed by Bruno Latour and his colleagues, offers one possible scaffolding for this enterprise in that it focusses explicitly on relay systems, on the tracing of linkages and associations between disparate elements (technologies, environments, discourses, institutions), as so many formattings of power.[102] ANT also offers a clear strategy for organising the archive to give priority to the potential and actual connections to be made between disparate items, rather than privileging their collation into fixed, a priori thematic or analytic categories.

ANT's current vogue comes from the fact that it is a methodology ideally suited to track the trans-local conduits of information through which globalised knowledge/power relations are disseminated. But let's be clear here: the internet, the chief engine of globalisation and the knowledge economy, is not and cannot be an archive. It may store unimaginably vast amounts of digitalised data and accelerate the flow of information, but it cannot do what a Living Archive does, which is to insert documents within a framework of interpretation, a narrative and community of practice that gives them new meaning.

As an example of the primacy of interpretation over platform, consider Albert Kahn's Archives of the Planet project. A self-made businessman with no formal academic training but an insatiable curiosity about the world, Kahn dispatched photographers to the four corners of the globe in search of documentary evidence about the impact of modern technologies on customary ways of life. He wanted to capture visually what was happening to ordinary people's lives on the cusp of momentous change in the 1930s.

This is the largest collection of early colour photographs in the world, but in scope and scale it cannot rival what is now available on Google Images. It nevertheless remains the only archive of its kind because the collection is inspired and organised around Kahn's internationalist vision.

At the level of archival practice, the challenge is how actively to socialise the process of acquiring, classifying, reading and re-presenting materials as an ongoing collaboration between donors, recipients and users conducted within a single interpretive community. For example, an archive could function as a platform for participatory action research by using collected campaigning material from the past as a learning resource for present-day groups involved in similar issues, thus building a bridge between different generations of activists.[103]

Here it is worth considering the role of the Living Archive as an interface between the Dissenting Academy and the communities whose causes it espouses. With the marginalisation of public intellectuals, their replacement by media-savvy academics with specialist expertise, the role of the scholar-activist has inevitably been pushed to the outer edges of cultural and intellectual life. The Living Archive may indeed be one of the few places where something like an intellectual commons can be sustained in which people without formal academic qualifications can work alongside professionals on anything like equal terms. Some of the most creative archivists turn out to be autodidacts, because the obsessionality which is often their hallmark can here be put to constructive use. At the same time we should not ignore the fact that the engagement of the Academy—and the hermeneutic archive—in community politics may actually intensify the gentrification of urban social movements, where those campaigning against the displacement of working-class and immigrant populations often include students, academics and creative professionals. It may also lead to the marginalisation of the popular archive as a site of collective remembrance and resistance. As we have seen in the discussion of the Black Cultural Archive, the location of archives in the social and cultural fabric of the city can be as important as what they do.

Curating the Anarchive

An archive, I have suggested, is a kind of map but one which neither simply reflects nor creates the territory whose features it delineates. Rather, as it imposes its own line of desire, it points towards hitherto unmapped waypoints created as it goes along. The idea that archives are improvisatory structures has been pioneered by Infoshop 56a in London and by the Interference Archive in New York.[104] The latter takes the form of an open-stacks collection which is continually being added to and contains many kinds of objects created by participants in social movements. This ever-changing assemblage of ephemera is used pedagogically to animate narratives about material cultures and political campaigns marginalised or ignored by mainstream institutions.

Yet improvisation is only one side of the story. The conservation of materials usually requires suitable storage facilities, trained staff, specialised equipment, and above all a long-term commitment. Where conservation is the main priority, we see the emergence of the dark archive. In London, for example, the archival repository of the Science Museum contains an enormous collection of industrial archaeology, many of the machines in impeccable working order, but they are unlikely to ever see the light of day in public exhibitions or become accessible to amateur communities of interest. The function of the dark archive is precisely to preserve these things from present use, to keep them in pristine condition against the deterioration of 'aging', so that they are available to some notional 'future generation'. It is a form of arche-cryonics, deep freezing the material culture of past, then burying it in the archive in the hope that at some unspecified future date it will be re-animated.

The balancing act between bonding and bridging in the accumulation of archival capital, between the capacity to respond proactively to emergent areas and the need to preserve and consolidate existing holdings is a perennial issue. One way of reconciling these conflicting priorities lies in exploring the notion of the *erratic but immersive archive* whose curation policy mirrors both senses of our mode of dwelling in the world: not just lingering over moments and materials that are usually skimmed or abridged, if not totally ignored, but also hop-skip-and-jumping over the major, already well-documented landmarks of, say, labour history or women's history in search of lost causes or hidden singularities that figure on a deeper map. The Living Archivist is no longer just a keeper of records but an agent provocateur of new knowledge following the hermeneutic trail, hunting for clues to unlock the stories hidden within the material. I propose to call this approach *anarchival*.[105]

The creative potential of the anarchive has been foregrounded by a pervasive shift from collection to curation as a defining practice.[106] The combined impact of contemporary museology, with its ever-more-spectacular displays of artefacts, and librarianship, with its fetishism of informational architecture linked to mnemo-technology, has been to load these quasi-aesthetic functions onto archival practice, while relegating the bureaucratic aspect of archiving to a secondary role within the museum and library itself. This inflation of curatorial capacity is partly a response to the threat of deskilling or deprofessionalisation associated with the advent of the open-source archive, the automation of routine processes of recordkeeping and information retrieval. But while these developments may make many semi-skilled forms of mental labour redundant, they expand and enhance the role of the archivist as someone who possesses the interpretive skills needed to make sense of all this raw data.

This curatorial turn in archival practice is mirrored by an archival turn in contemporary art practice. Artists raid all manner of archives, official and unofficial, populist and hermeneutic, in search of material from which to construct visual narratives and installations. Out of these lost-and-found images and objects scavenged from here, there and everywhere, is created a meshwork of citation and juxtaposition, often presented in a quasi-archival form and challenging dominant interpretations of the past. Sam Durant, for example, employs photographs, drawings, Xerox collages, sculpture and installation to sample the history of popular music, 1960s social activism, modern dance, Japanese garden design, self-help literature and do-it-yourself home improvements. Sometimes there is a very specific focus, for example the deconstruction of the received history of American involvement in Vietnam, and his interventions are always to the point, as in his witty comment on roots radical historiography.[107] Reviewing his work, Hal Foster says that Durant 'presents his archive materials as active, even unstable, open to eruptive returns and entropic collapses, stylistic repackaging and critical revisions'.[108]

At first sight, then, it seems as if we have here a paradigm for the methodology of the anarchive. Yet further consideration of artwork created in this idiom opens up some doubts. However interesting the visual research, and however dramatic its re-presentation, the essential technique is that of the digital mash-up. The elaborate meta-narrative woven around these pieces, often cluttered with post-structuralist jargon, attempts to sketch in some art-historical hinterland, such as Kurt Schwitters's Dadaist collage or John Heartfield's photomontage, but these 'authorising' references are not really integral to the actual work. Oscillating undecidably between de- and re-historicising their references, these exotic assemblages give a spectacular aesthetic gloss to the chaotic synchronicity of contemporary capitalist culture with its shimmering circuits of visual seduction. The declared intent may be to interrupt, subvert or 'detourn' the flow, but the medium remains a message too caught up in its own visual rhetoric to offer more than a vacuous or disingenuous critique. These are not true inventories in Gramsci's or Benjamin's sense; they are all map and no territory. It is no coincidence that one central reference point for this trend in conceptual art is Foucault's formulation of the archive as an a priori of knowledge, an epistemological paradigm entirely abstracted from any actual archival practice.

What this archival turn in art does show is that there is no ducking the challenge of digital technology to cultural memory. There is a very real danger that the software programmes needed to read older digitalised documents are rapidly becoming obsolete, so that large amounts of social data stored in virtual archives will eventually be unretrievable. An ironic complement to the process of 'tomecide'.

Perhaps no one, apart from future historians of popular culture, will lose any sleep if 'bit rot' attacks the instant archiving of everyday life which our digital devices accomplish, or even if the ever-expanding inventories of our ever-accelerating production of texts stored on our personal computers or via Dropbox become dysfunctional. But there is a broader issue here.

It used to be technophobes who proclaimed that digital culture was responsible for the end of civilisation as they knew it. But now these same concerns are being voiced by digital activists themselves. For example, they are beginning to argue that the so called 'smart city' agenda, the corporate techno-utopia being supposedly created by artificial intelligence and the internet of things will actually lead to the creation of cities without collective memoryscapes. And this concern is not confined to activists. There are signs that many citizens of cyberspace are beginning to rebel against the 'quantified self' created through social media.[109] The fetishism of curation is not confined to the so-called creative class. Its application to everything from T-shirts to lists of algorithmically sampled music on Spotify speaks to the pervasive desire to wrest some sense of personal signature and enduring life-historical value from—or impose such a sense upon—what is otherwise just another consumerist mash-up. There may be more common ground between the epistemic priorities of the professional archivist and the ontological needs of the amateur collector than either have dared to suspect or admit.

In any case the Living Anarchive has to establish a new partnership with the spontaneous memorialisations of the do-it-yourself chronicler of passing events whose videos and blogs provide such graphic documentation of the political events and the cultural scene. If Mass Observation were to be re-invented for the digital age, its network of correspondents, now renamed and trained up as 'citizen social scientists', would be responding to the 'directives' on their smart phones and sending in images, texts and audio recordings in their thousands to be uploaded into the archive.[110] How far they could then be employed in the interpretation of this mass of material—it would amount to a huge but still qualitative data set—while working alongside professional anthropologists, is a moot point.[111] Even the most libertarian, open-source projects tend to consolidate existing patterns of intellectual and cultural capital if only because most donors and downloaders of material are drawn from the ranks of the intelligentsia and others who have a vested interest in the dissemination of information. An effective challenge to the intellectual property rights embedded in the routine online archival operations of the global knowledge economy, and codified in law, would require a level of digital activism hard to sustain over a long period.

For the time being, at any rate, the virtual archive is no substitute for the real thing. We still need the hermeneutic archive as a *lieu de mémoire* in its own right, a place with its own unique characteristics where we can get hands-on experience in reading original documents, have face-to-face encounters with staff, and meet our fellow researchers over lunch to discuss common enthusiasms, share the latest gossip and generally sustain the intellectual commons.[112] And we still need the popular archive as a rallying point for disparate groups who would otherwise lack the resource to connect their concerns to other traditions of struggle. Above all, as I have argued, we need to develop more hybrid anarchives that combine both these functions. Finally, let's not forget that archives are brought alive by the people who use them. They expand or contract, change direction or emphasis, under the impress of external circumstance and internal constraint. Paradoxically this is a history that is rarely documented by the archive itself.

Not Everyone Will Be Taken into the Future

We are all time travellers and we also know that time's arrow, all appearances to the contrary, does not fly in one direction or follow a straight line. If we live long enough to come from a place that has become a foreign country simply because it no longer issues passports recognised by the current arbiters of significance, then its remembrance, of necessity, becomes an act of trespass, criss-crossing all those invisible lines in the sands of time which contemporary historians have drawn to get their bearings: the 1960s, the Thatcher years, the Digital Age, the Post-War, the Post-Millennium, the Noughties, Generation X—so many fixed points of reference that strive to capture the Zeitgeist but usually fail to engage the actual periodicities that inform the unfolding of real lives or events. To trace the erratic course of biographies and histories at the contingent points where they intersect to personal and political effect, and to configure those points into new networks of meaning, must surely be what the Living Archive is all about. This does *not* require an attempt to reanimate grand narratives that have fallen into disrepute or lost their purchase on the present. It is *not* a project to revive oral traditions as an authentic alternative to mnemo-technology in transmitting political or cultural heritage to a new generation. Nor is it about promoting the 'pop-up archive' as a form of digital guerrilla warfare against the tyranny of the internet. So what does it involve?

I want to discuss some work which seems to me to exemplify the approach I am arguing for and which is produced by the desire to create imaginative platforms on which to re-present the voices and stories of ordinary people in ways that challenge the official public record. The first body of work is by installation artists. Christian Boltanski is driven by the need as the child of Ukrainian Jews to address the dark side of European history. In a number of projects he has explored the multiple layering of memory by creating imaginary archives in which the material presence of real lives is powerfully evoked yet haunted by intimations of their absence, and often by their entrapment in a traumatic and unrepresentable past. The shadow of the Nazi Holocaust and other genocides falls heavily across these pieces.

For his purposes Boltanski often works with photographs collected from ordinary and often ephemeral sources. Rather than taking original photographs to use in his installations, he finds and re-photographs every-day documents—passport photographs, school portraits, newspaper pictures, and family albums—with a view to reframing them within a back story that is suggested but requires more research by the spectator to be fully spelt out. Boltanski is interested in what he calls 'small memory': 'little things: trivia, jokes . . . because often when someone dies, that memory disappears. Yet that "small memory" is what makes people different from one another, unique. These memories are very fragile; I wanted to save them'.[113] He calls many of his works 'inventories', and indeed they are inventories in the Gramscian sense, albeit inflected by a Benjaminesque melancholy. In *The Children of Dijon*, for example, dozens of photos of children's faces, deeply blurred and simply framed, are hung all over a wall, each illuminated by little bulbs (the only light source) whose flexes trail nakedly between the pictures. This is archive as catacomb/mortuary/shrine, and we have to discover for ourselves what exactly happened to send these children to a premature death.

In a statement which could be read as a manifesto for the anarchival project, Boltanski writes:

> An artwork is open—it is the spectators looking at the work who make the piece, using their own background. A lamp in my work might make you think of a police interrogation, but it is also religious, like a candle. At the same time it alludes to a precious painting, with a single light shining on it. There are many ways of looking at the work. It has to be 'unfocused' somehow so that everyone can recognize something of their own history when viewing it.[114]

In their installations the Russians Ilya and Emilia Kabakov explore a different but no less fraught history, that of everyday life under Stalinism. Whereas Boltanski only puts himself in his work to distance or problematise his identity as an artist, the Kabakovs are present only indirectly and through fictional characters (The Untalented Artist, The Garbage Man, White) that serve as their always ambiguous avatars and often as a reflection of the various false personas artists had to adopt in order to ingratiate themselves with the regime. Their declared aim is to chart the utopian impulse as it manifests itself in ordinary Russians' day-to-day struggle to survive. And not just to survive but if possible to escape or transcend the bleakness and petty repressions of the Communist regime with its seedy but seductive form of 'caring authoritarianism'. Their paintings often make ironic reference to the legacy of socialist realism and its impact on Russian art; the major installations all focus on the challenge of remembering a past which was officially—and artistically—represented as leading to a glorious future but which in reality was filled with endless privation and humiliation. *The Man Who Flew into Space from His Apartment* shows a large room plastered with official posters extolling the virtues of Soviet life, but with a large hole in the ceiling where the occupant has made a spectacular exit in the quest for a better world, presumably on another planet. Many of the Kabakovs' rooms are filled with everyday domestic objects, piled up in heaps or floating in the air along with scraps of conversation, which evoke the cramped conditions of communal living in shared apartments. Ilya Kabokov writes about his *dingpolitik* in the following terms: 'For me these "things" represented a concentration of distinctive psychological feelings. I felt as if pushed, squashed into that world, filled with mystery and emptiness where everything was suspended in silent, uncomfortable anticipation. Everything was pushed into that world only halfway, as if into a suitcase that won't close'.[115]

A similar claustrophobia is induced by *Labyrinth*, which consists of a fifty-metre-long corridor with rows of framed images/texts conveying the life story of his mother. He writes: 'When I think about that world in which my mother's life passed, about the condensed image of it, what arises in my imagination is a long and semi-dark corridor twisted like a labyrinth, where behind each new turn there is not a bright exit glimmering in the distance but just the same grubby floor, the same gray, dusty, poorly painted wall illuminated by weak, 40-watt bulbs'.[116]

The experience of navigating this installation is nothing if not immersive. Craning their necks to read the short extracts from the memoir perched precariously enough on top of each frame while attempting to decode the often-faded photographs, spectators are assailed by contradictory emotions: admiration for the mother's fortitude in dealing with the many misfortunes she suffered, never allowing herself a moment of self-pity; boredom or exhaustion at the remorseless quality of the reality being depicted; bewilderment at the sheer density and complexity of the narrative, which mirrors the experience of a whole generation of Russians; impatience to reach the end of the labyrinth and escape from the stultifying bleakness of this environment into a brighter world; and panic that no way out can ever be found.

In this way the installation simulates the living memoryscape of the long transition from Soviet Communism, and its deadening effect.[117] But it also evokes the paranoid fantasy of the archival researcher of getting lost in the corridors of knowledge/power, stifled by the dust and dead weight of the past. An object lesson, then, in what the Living Anarchist has to avoid at all costs.

The second body of work which I want to discuss is by two oral historians who have developed a distinctive and innovative archival methodology. The first, Alessandro Portelli, has explored the political mythologies created around particular events of great significance for the Left, among them the mass killing by Fascists of a whole village for supporting the Italian partisans in the Second World War; the murder of an Italian trade unionist; the clash between left-wing militants and the police in Rome in 1968; and the struggles of a coal-mining community against exploitation and worse in Harlan County, USA.[118] Portelli examines the memory politics that come into play around these different instances of class conflict, and how stories are constructed and continually revised to sustain particular ideological positions. He is especially alert to the tropes that are mobilised to give imaginative life and relevance to these accounts and shows how a revisionary process is intrinsic to the process of consensual validation in popular democratic struggles but is inimical to any kind of authoritarian or corporatist politics, whether practised by Communist parties or by the state.

Portelli's work belongs to the hermeneutic tradition in European literature and philosophy which has strong but critical links to Marxism and the ideas of Gramsci. My second exemplar, the late Studs Terkel, came from a Left populist tradition of political and intellectual dissent embedded in working-class, Jewish, Italian and other minority ethnic cultures in the USA.[119] His heroes were the Wobblies, Woody Guthrie and James Agee rather than Gramsci and Bloch. He set out to document the key common experiences of the American people in the twentieth century, experiences of mass unemployment and the Great Depression, of the Second World War and its aftermath, of social inequalities governed by divisions of class and race, of the pleasures of the working life and the travails of community. His great gift is to get people talking about their lives in context and to bring their testimonies together into a collective statement about the major fault lines than run through American society. There is no meta-narrative in his books, no overarching interpretative frame, only a certain implication of argument in his selection and juxta-position of texts. One of Terkel's recurrent themes is the principle of hope sustaining everyday struggles for a better life and a more just society, a principle both embodied in and betrayed by the American Dream. He is as interested in the quest for meaning and recognition which animates the moves made by street gangs in the black ghetto as in the articles of faith which motivate political activists, jazz musicians and dissidents of every kind.[120]

What can the Living Anarchivist learn from these models? First, the importance of establishing clearly and at the outset the moral compass and political scope of the project; and, second, the need to avoid foreclos-ing the sociological imagination of informants by pigeonholing them and jumping to conclusions about where their stories 'fit' into the wider scheme of things. The second point, which mitigates the risk of foreclo-sure inherent in the first, is perhaps the more important. There is always the danger of a *dingpolitik* of the archive becoming just another exercise in reification. The very notion of a 'deposit' intimates the inert quasi-geolog-ical stratification of ossified material into different levels of significance, a sedimentation of the historical process into fixed, hierarchical layers of meaning. This in turn underwrites what we might call the 'archaeologi-cal fantasy', the idea that that by digging ever deeper into anarchive we will discover the historical truth. In fact what we might just discover is the foundational myth of the archive itself, its Other Scene. For there is an aura of the uncanny about the ghosts in the machinery of the archive—about all those material and textual traces of the lives of the dead, mapping unknown territory where, as researchers venturing in, we are at risk of being trapped in an immersive world, and of becoming strangers to ourselves even as we strive to provide an animated portrait of times and places other than our own.[121] Arlette Farge has written movingly of this predicament: 'The archive is excessive and overwhelming, like a spring tide, an avalanche or a flood. This comparison with unpredictable forces is not arbitrary. When working in the archive you will often find yourself thinking of this exploration as a dive, a submersion, even a drowning.... You feel yourself immersed in something vast, oceanic'.[122]

The museological ambitions of the archivist certainly tend to pull curatorial practice towards a form of cultural taxidermy, if not cryonics. That is why I have stressed the importance of the erratic, the continual need to improvise and destabilise meanings in the midst of an enterprise that is so vitally concerned to find safe anchorage. Italo Calvino, in this as so much else, provides us with the moral compass we need:

> The inferno of the living is not something that will be; if there is one, it is what is already here, the inferno where we live every day, that we form by being together. There are two ways to escape suffering it. The first is easy for many: accept the inferno and become such a part of it that you can no longer see it. The second is risky and demands constant vigilance and apprehension: seek and learn to recognize who and what, in the midst of inferno, are not inferno, then make them endure, give them space.[123]

The Arc of Memory

The anarchival standpoint I have been arguing for is grounded in personal experience. When my adoptive son died recently from alcoholism while still in his early thirties, he left behind a chaotic jumble of things, most of them in a van filled with books, booze and dirty clothes in which he lived for last terrible month of his life. He also left behind two young teenage sons, and we had to decide how best to create a small archive that in the future might support and sustain their own memoryscape of growing up with their dad.

Of course my partner and I had lots of photographs of Stephen's time with us, starting from when he first came to us at the age of eight, his teenage years, and then as a young father. He also came with an official life story book, a visual archive of the key figures in his early life, including his mother who abandoned him at eighteen months old, his various foster carers and social workers, and the 'aunties' from the children's home where he mostly lived. We decided to borrow a device from adoption counselling and construct a 'memory box' containing various objects which were important to Stephen at various stages in his life: his teddy bear, his guitar, photo albums, his Arsenal shirt, his favourite cap, his drawings and cartoons (he was a gifted draughtsman), his workmen's tools (he was a skilled craftsman), books that were important to him when he became a student and the essays he wrote, not to forget his exercise gear. Rather than simply giving these things directly to his two sons, as mementoes, which might have raised issues about who was to have what, we decided to keep them together, until such time as they were ready to work through their feelings about their relationship with Stephen. For the moment they were too angry and upset by what had happened to deal with

This photo shows part of the backdrop of Goshka Macuga's 2013 work *Death of Marxism, Women of All Lands Unite*, a large wool tapestry that drapes partially onto the floor.

legacy issues. His eldest son in particular blocked off the whole situation, while the younger one was able to begin to mourn, and this inequality of response has continued over the past few years. The two brothers seem embarked on very different trajectories, and this will inevitably shape how they eventually engage with this material.

The memory box is thus at the moment a kind of ark, a way of keeping Stephen's things safe, not as holy relics or props for consecrating his memory to some idealised narrative of his life but rather as a container of hopes for their transformation into a Living Archive through what his sons will one day make of it. In other words this little archive is still in its latency period, inert but waiting to be discovered, to have its manifest content sifted and transposed into a new and different idiom of remembrance. All the objects have stories attached to them, but so far these belong only to my partner and me, as Stephen's adoptive parents. Our hope is that one day the box will be opened and the contents support a conversation in which we share and exchange the stories they evoke with Stephen's sons. In this way it may be possible for them to integrate their father's life, with all its ups and down, into the ongoing story of their own. Of course this may not happen—it may just be too painful a process—in which case the box will become a coffin of buried memories and entombed hopes. If it does work, however, this particular archival project will have lived up to our expectations and, having served its purpose, could be safely put aside and forgotten.

In the shadow of Marx's monumental tomb in Highgate Cemetery, amid so many luminaries of the revolutionary Left,[124] is a small plaque to a local resident, a Mr Griffiths, who was famous only to his family and friends for his love of poetry as well as for his devotion to improving the lot of his fellow working man. According to his epitaph he 'fell asleep', and his life has remained dormant and unsung ever since. Those who come to worship at the shrine of Marxism tend not to notice this little overgrown plot or consider for a moment what its overlooking might tell us about the fate of the international communist movement in the twentieth century. But it is the unearthing of stories such as this which, it seems to me, allows us to untangle the knots tied by the ruses of political remembrance—and give the Living Left Anarchive its purchase on the future.

Postscript: The Politics of False Memory in the Age of 'Post-Truth'

The central assumption running through much of my argument is that the Left needs to get its archival act together to face the challenges of the present political conjuncture. Yet it cannot have escaped the reader's attention that the need to meet the challenge in the field of memory politics from the alt-right has thus far not been addressed.

In Britain the hard-line Brexiteers have made much play with the idea that leaving the European Union is a prime way to put the 'Great' back into Britain by reasserting its archival identity as a maritime nation and regaining control of the cultural heritage entailed in 'our island story'.[125] In the case of Trump, the mantra 'make America great again' played to a sense of long-lost glory days which resonated widely enough to get him elected. For the blue-collar working class in the Rust Belt it promised a return to the job securities of Fordism; for rural 'white trash' and small-town America it offered a revival of 'good ol' boy culture' laced with a strong dose of Southern Comfort and Confederate pride.[126] Trump's countless other supporters included even immigrants, who found that his chauvinist rhetoric somehow left them enough leeway for dissociation, scope to draw the line of exclusion under their own feet while feeling good about themselves as pursuers of the American Dream.

The appeal to revitalise the present state of the nation and gain purchase on the future by returning to the status quo ante is of course a typical retro-modernist conceit. In the case of both the Brexiteers and the Trumpistas it is part of a decisive shift from bridging to bonding as a populist strategy for strengthening the social capital of communitarianism against the perceived dominance of a cosmopolitan elite.

What has been less observed as part of this process is the way the populist anarchive has been appropriated by the libertarian alt-right and mobilised both to attack the credibility of evidence-based research and to insinuate new, entirely undemocratic and sometimes openly authoritarian criteria for what should be remembered and celebrated about the past.

Within this ideological frame the anarchival impulse can take a number of different forms. The improvisatory dimension is now notoriously associated with Trump's governance by tweet. This has created an erratic information flow in which there is a total absence of any logical or narratological principle of sequencing, so that it can only be archived as a series of disconnected and often contradictory bits of information with very low redundancy. It is certainly a good way to keep the commentariat on the edge of their seats—they never quite know what is coming next! At the same time, thematically, the message has very high redundancy, involving a continual reiteration of the same catch phrases, which makes the task of indexing this discourse an algorithmic doddle.

Where the alt-right anarchive distinguishes itself most strongly from the kind of Living Archive I have been arguing for is in its subsumption of past and future in a hysterical present. This entails an absolute disavowal of the archive's revisionary impetus, and the deployment of 'eternal truths' and a priori moralistic criteria for dealing with current events. 'Fake news' is whatever fails to conform to those specifications. This presentism is hysterical in the sense that it is a manic defence against the recognition of the often painful back stories and contradictory trajectories which govern contemporary reality, and it serves to buttress entirely fictional facticities. So we have whole archives devoted to documenting 'what if' propositions such as 'What if Britain had never joined the EU?' or 'What if the Confederate South had won the Civil War?'

'What if' propositions all too easily slide into 'as if' actions. The fictional archive, once released from any commitment to represent, however allegorically, the always provisional truth about its own conditions of existence, becomes a willing enough accomplice for projects that seek to remake the world in the image of the archivist. This invariably involves the magical righting of both real and imaginary wrongs while systematically blurring any distinction between them.

The populist alt-right anarchive provides ammunition for countless projects of revenge bearing on hidden wounds of class, gender, generation and race, and for this purpose draws on the everyday experience of personal slight as well as selective historical testimony. The target, as always in populist projects, is the cultural, intellectual and political elites who, in this context, are perceived to control the official archive and to hold the keys to the corridors of knowledge power, whether in the academy or government.

The memoryscapes evoked in this project, whether built around daydreams of patriarchy or white supremacy, of empire or world domination, all evoke a mythical once-upon-a-time Golden Age. They are not just the stuff of nightmares for the rest of us—they represent a concerted attempt to turn the historical clock back so as 'normalise' distorted visions of omniscience and to legitimate, even glorify, the sordid attempt to settle old scores through acts of symbolic and sometimes physical violence. In the process we are invited to subscribe to a politics of false memory, often as an oath of allegiance to party, nation or state, and to forget the whole history of our struggles, generation after generation, to make the society we live in and the world at large a better, fairer, more interesting and joyful place. Against this background the task of the Living Left Archive should need no further spelling out.

Notes

1   See Ian Cobain, *The History Thieves: Secrecy, Lies and the Shaping of the Modern Nation* (2016).

2   The members of the Apostles Club at various times included Alfred Lord Tennyson, Maynard Keynes, Lytton Strachey, G.E. Moore, Rupert Brooke, Guy Burgess and Anthony Blunt. It was confined to students and fellows of Kings and St Johns, the most elite colleges of this elite university.

3   The concept of an open archive was originally posed in a successful campaign by adoptees to gain access to information about their birth parents and the circumstances of their adoption. Questions of access have also been raised in campaigns by the families of 'the disappeared'—those kidnapped or murdered by political regimes. It could be argued, however, that secrecy and control of access are not confined to state or corporate institutions, or to authoritarian regimes, but are also a constitutive feature in the history of the archive in civil societies within liberal democracies. The campaign for transparency in governance has led to archiving procedures being built into administrative procedures, but access to them remains a site of contestation. Just how sensitive the issue has become is evidenced by the furore during the 2016 presidential election over Hillary Clinton's use of her private email address for communications that potentially contained classified information and/or should have formed part of her governmental archive as secretary of state.

4   For a discussion of this point, see Achille Mbembe's article 'The Power of the Archive and Its Limits' in *Refiguring the Archive* (2013)

5   The Guild Socialists were not immune to 'Merrie England' mythology and in their quest for historical precedents for their model of popular democratic self-governing organisation in both the workplace and civil society, they seized on the mediaeval Moot as prefigurative of their vision. See G.D.H. Cole, *Guild Socialism Restated* (1920).

6   See Walter Benjamin, *The Arcades Project*, trans. Howard Eiland and Kevin McLaughlin (1999). Also Walter Benjamin, *Archive: Images, Texts, Signs*, ed. Ursula Marx et al., trans. Esther Leslier (2008).

7   See my 'A Place Beyond Belief: Hysterical Materialism and the Making of East 20', in Phil Cohen and Paul Watt, eds., *London 2012 and the Post-Olympics City: A Hollow Legacy?* (2017).

8   The term refers to the diffusion and internalisation of new mobile technologies of surveillance and regulation associated with the development of digital culture, which both atomises and individualises patterns of public behaviour and massifies/reifies them. This thesis was first developed by Gilles Deleuze in a short article in *October* and has subsequently been taken up by a number of cultural commentators including Loïc Wacquant, who has focussed on how the control society has been mobilised in the micromanagement of the urban poor. See *Punishing the Poor: The Neoliberal Government of Social Insecurity* (2009). Arjun Appadurai's 2003 analysis, while recognising this negative aspect of digital technology also stresses the potential of what he calls its 'prosthetic socialities' to create new platforms of collective aspiration and memory.

9   See Phil Cohen, *Reading Room Only: Memoir of a Radical Bibliophile* (2013) and 'Recognizing in the Inferno That Which Is Not: Reflections on Memoir Writing'. *History Workshop Journal* 74 (1): 2012.

10   See Guy Standing, *The Precariat: The New Dangerous Class* (2011).

11   See, for example, Luc Boltanski and Eve Chiappello, *The New Spirit of Capitalism* (2007).

12   See Thomas Frank, *The Conquest of the Cool* (1997) and Dick Pountain and David Robins, *Cool Rules* (2000) for two complementary critiques.

13   Consider, for example, The Subculture Archives in London's Carnaby Street. This shop, located in what was once upon a time the showcase of the Sixties teenage style industry, features exhibitions of postwar British youth culture from the Teds, Mods and Rockers through to the Beats, Hippies and Punks as a means of promoting retro-fashion. In this way a consumerist version of a 'Living Archive' is manufactured out of what are essentially 'granny fashions'. For discussion of this phenomenon, see S. Blackman and M. Kempson, *The Subcultural Imagination* (2016)

14   Theodore Roszak's *The Making of a Counter Culture* (1969) remains the classic positive reading, while Paul Berlant in *A Tale of Two Utopias* (2007) offers a more nuanced account of the trajectory of the 1968 generation based on a series of comparative case studies tracing the political and ideological legacy right up to the Velvet Revolution of 1989. For a more theoretically sophisticated analysis of the political legacies and cultural mythologies surrounding the May 'évènements', see Luisa Passerini, *Autobiography of a Generation: Italy 68* (1996), which explores links between the Italian student movement and what was happening in Paris.

15   See, for example, the anthology *1963: The Year of the Revolution: How Youth Changed the World with Music, Arts and Fashion* (2013). 'You Say You Want a Revolution', a recent major exhibition at the Victoria and Albert Museum

in London took a similar line (Broackes and Marsh, eds., 2016). A somewhat more sanguine version of the same story can be found in Jon Savage's many writings on Sixties youth culture and its aftermath. George Melly's *Revolt into Style* and Jeff Nuttall's *Bomb Culture* are entertaining if largely anecdotal accounts of the cultural politics of the British underground scene. Charles Radcliffe's two-volume memoir *Don't Start Me Talkin'* is an exhaustive blow-by-blow insider account of the scene and its multiple forms of cultural and political activity. Barry Miles, who ran Indica Books, one of the seminal 'scenes' of the London underground culture has now become its chief archivist. See, for example, his *In the Sixties* (2002) and *London Calling: A Countercultural History of London since 1945* (2010).

16   See Tariq Ali, *Street Fighting Years: An Autobiography of the Sixties* (2005) and Ronald Fraser, *1968: A Student Generation in Revolt* (1988).

17   Herbert Marcuse, *Eros and Civilisation* (1972)

18   BIT was founded in 1968 by John Hopkins, the legendary *animateur* of the London underground scene, as an information centre for the alternative society, and under Nick Albery's direction evolved into an organiser of free festivals and other events. Release was founded by Caroline Coon as a legal advice and support centre, spearheading a campaign to decriminalise recreational drug use.

19   See, for example, Alexander Vasudevan, *The Autonomous City: A History of Urban Squatting* (2017).

20   See chapter 1 of my *Rethinking the Youth Question* (1998)

21   '*Détournement*' was developed as a strategy of cultural action by the French Situationists in the early 1960s and has subsequently influenced or been adopted by numerous artists and others who want to disrupt the consumer spectacle. The word can mean 'perversion' in a transitive sense, as in *détournement de mineurs*, the sexual seduction of minors; cf. also *détournement de fonds*, or embezzling. In its Situationist usage, the term suggests the perversion of the seductive power of the Spectacle. *Détournement* has often erroneously been seen as prefiguring postmodernist 'appropriation'. But the concept is not about a bricolage of borrowed elements repurposed to create a parody, pastiche, or a form of ironic plagiarism. Rather it involves some kind of performative act interrupting a chain of signifiers in order not just to 'deconstruct' their conventional reading but to subvert it by substituting an alternative chain of associations. The concept has influenced a variety of practices such culture jamming, adbusting and 'subvertisements', in which the text and images of consumer messages (e.g., Nike's) are altered for this purpose. Increasingly the technique has been recuperated—a mirror concept developed by Guy Debord to explain how radical practices are neutralised and subsumed under the dominant ideology, for example Che Guevara's iconic image serving to sell T-shirts or cigars. Slavoj Žižek has picked up on this phenomenon in his usual acute but lopsided way, arguing that *détournement* as currently practised by artists, by creating distance from the sign systems of capitalism, represents a fantasy of transgression which hides an actual complicity. Naomi Klein makes the same point in *No Logo*

(2008), her study of branding, when she points out that corporate imagineering frequently makes use of 'subversive' images to give an edge to its products. In the context of memory politics, using the dominant archival or curatorial forms to challenge the content of the public record is similarly subject to recuperation. Consider, for instance, the recent exhibition on punk culture organised by the British Library (2016).

22 Ron Bailey, *The Squatters* (1973).

23 Samuel Fuller, *144 Piccadilly* (1969).

24 See Todd Gitlin's account in *Years of Hope, Days of Rage* (1993).

25 Street Aid was based initially in Soho and offered free legal advice; it was linked to the Muggins Trust, a social housing project for homeless young people set up in memory of one of the street communards who committed suicide after a bad acid trip.

26 For example, in Britain in 2015 we have seen the reprinting of the 1968 May Day Manifesto, the revival of the Anti-University, the establishment of an archive of the sometime left-leaning Greater London Council, and a fiftieth-anniversary edition of *International Times* which looks and reads almost exactly like the original version of British Hippiedom's flagship newspaper.

27 See T.J. Clark, 'For a Left without a Future', *New Left Review* 74 (2012).

28 For discussion of Gramsci's maxim and its contemporary relevance, see my article 'The Centre Will Not Hold: On Changing Principles of Hope', *Soundings* 60: 2015. For a discussion of the political and cultural manipulation of hope, see Lauren Berlant, *Cruel Optimism* (2011), and for its wider philosophical ramifications, see Terry Eagleton, *Hope without Optimism* (2015).

29 Here, for example is George Orwell writing about miners: 'Nearly all of them have the most noble bodies; wide shoulders tapering to slender supple waists and small pronounced buttocks and sinewy thighs, with not an ounce of waste flesh anywhere.' Quoted in John Sutherland *Orwell's Nose: A Pathological Biography* (2016). For an overview of the British literati's view of the working class, see John Carey, *The Intellectuals and the Masses: Pride and Prejudice in the Literary Intelligentsia, 1880–1939* (2003).

30 See Studs Terkel, *Hope Dies Last: Making a Difference in an Indifferent World* (2005).

31 The distinction between anamnesis and hypomnesis, was first made in Plato's *Phaedrus*. For the Greeks the crucial distinction was between spoken and written forms of remembrance, from the immediate transmission of memories in everyday speech to its exteriorised and publicly mediated forms. This distinction has been taken up by both Jacques Derrida in his essay 'Plato's Pharmacy' and Bernard Stiegler in *For a New Critique of Political Economy* (2013), especially in relation to the role of digital archives, which are in the process of automating mnemo-technologies. The social historian Pierre Nora, drawing on the pioneering work of Maurice Halbwachs, argues that the primary process of collective memory work remains anamnesis, but that this has increasingly been supplanted by the secondary process of hypomnesis, in the form of rituals of public commemoration which both simulate and hollow out the more immediate and intimate (and for him more authentic)

forms of memory work. For a thoroughgoing critique of Nora's position, see Bill Schwarz, 'Memory, Temporality, Modernity: Les lieux de mémoire' in Sussanah Radstone and Bill Schwarz, eds., *Memory: History, Theories, Debates* (2010).

32 Suttee is a now obsolete Hindu funeral custom in which a widow immolates herself on her husband's pyre or commits suicide in another fashion shortly after his death. It is a literal enactment of what is otherwise recognised as a purely symbolic act—mourning as a social death in which the widow dons 'widow's weeds' and withdraws from social intercourse for a stipulated period.

33 Freud's famous essay 'Mourning and Melancholia' (1917) remains the touchstone of contemporary debates. There is today a whole therapeutic industry of bereavement counselling built around Elisabeth Kübler-Ross's five-stage model of mourning, which is a loose extrapolation from Freud's schema (Kübler-Ross, 1989). The normative aspects of this model have become a self-fulfilling prophecy while those whose cultures of mourning deviate from it come to be regarded as sociopathic. In contrast Judith Butler in *Precarious Life* (2004) has elaborated an ethical theory of mourning which draws on Melanie Klein's model of object attachment and loss and stresses structures of symbolic recognition, debt and reparation as the key dynamic. Butler critiques the politicisation of mourning, or rather its instrumental subsumption under nationalist or communitarian ideologies. The concept of 'active mourning' had been developed in order to suggest that the experience of loss can be productive and shareable. See David L. Eng and David Kazanjian (eds.), *Loss: The Politics of Mourning* (2002), especially the two chapters on 'Left Melancholy' by Charity Scribner and Wendy Brown.

34 Stephen Lawrence was a black teenager murdered in a racist attack in London in 1993. A campaign to bring his murderers to justice was launched by his family led by his mother, Doreen Lawrence, who became a national figure and was eventually elevated to the House of Lords. The campaign widened its focus to include the institutionalised racism of the Metropolitan Police, their mishandling of the enquiry, their attempt to smear the Lawrence family and the subsequent cover-up. The campaign changed the terms of public debate on race and the police in Britain and led to the partial amendment of the law of double jeopardy. This in turn led to two of the murderers, who originally had their cases dismissed for lack of evidence, being retried, found guilty and given long sentences. See Brian Cathcart, *The Case of Stephen Lawrence* (2000).

35 See Denis O'Hearn, *Bobby Sands: Nothing but an Unfinished Song* (2016).

36 For an analysis of inheritance as a social and symbolic order of customary practices spanning relations of kinship and community, as well as the transfer of material assets, see E.P. Thompson, 'The Grid of Inheritance' (1976), and for its function as a principle of periodisation and predicament thrown across the life course, see my *Material Dream: Maps and Territories in the Un/making of Modernity* (forthcoming).

37 See Alastair Bonnett, *The Geography of Nostalgia: Global and Local Perspectives on Modernity and Loss* (2016).

38 There is now an extensive literature on the marginalisation of the manual working class. For the UK, see for example Linda MacDowell, *Redundant Masculinities* (2011); Owen Jones, *Chavs: the Demonization of the Working Class* (2011); and Michael Collins, *The Likes of Us: A Biography of the White Working Class* (2006). For the USA, Ruy Teixeira and Joel Rogers, *America's Forgotten Majority: Why the White Working Class Still Matters* (2000).

39 Kristin Ross, *May 68 and Its Afterlives* (2002) provides the best analysis of the biographical after-effects of the counter culture.

40 Michael Mitterauer, *A History of Youth* (2004) and Alexander Mitscherlich, *Society without the Father* (1969).

41 On the home front and its collective memoryscape, see Angus Calder, *The People's War* (1997) and Joanna Bourke, *The Second World War: A People's History* (2001) for the UK, and Studs Terkel, *"The Good War"* (1986) for the USA.

42 This argument is developed in David Rieff, *In Praise of Forgetting* (2016).

43 From a classic psychoanalytical perspective the concept of trauma is linked to Freud's archaeological model of the unconscious and the notion of a 'return of the repressed'. Some incident in the present triggers the deeply repressed memory and leads to a symbolic reenactment of the original traumatising event. However, Freud's concept of *nachträglichkeit*, often translated as 'after-shock', 'deferred action', or *après-coup*, suggests a less linear and mechanistic model of causality, whereby the sedimentation of a traumatic historical event in a partial and tolerable memory (which may be shared and even archived) allows for its continuing unconscious representation, as in dreams and psychosomatic symptoms, and this material may erupt into consciousness whenever the subject is stressed through some quite unrelated circumstance. The construction of 'posttraumatic stress disorder' as a clinical category has created an aetiology that bypasses the Freudian Unconscious in favour of a cognitivist/behavioural model of causality in mental health. There is now a vast literature on this subject, but for an anthology of recent debates see Paul Antze and Michael Lambek (eds.), *Tense Past: Cultural Essays in Trauma and Memory* (2016). For a discussion of the role of visual archives in documenting traumatic memoryscapes, see Ulrich Baer, *Spectral Evidence: The Photography of Trauma* (2002).

44 See John Lennon and Malcolm Foley, *Dark Tourism* (2000).

45 For a discussion of these issues, see Marianne Hirsch, *The Generation of Postmemory: Writing and Visual Culture after the Holocaust* (2012), James E. Young, *The Texture of Memory: Holocaust Memorials and Meaning* (1993), and Ulrich Baer, *Spectral Evidence: The Photography of Trauma* (2002).

46 The oral history movement in Britain was pioneered by Raphael Samuels and the *History Workshop Journal*. It was initially linked to Ruskin College, Oxford, which was affiliated to the labour movement, but its remit quickly expanded to cover women's history, gay history, immigrant and minority ethnic histories, indeed every aspect of social and cultural history in which oral testimony and autobiographical writing provided an essential supplement to archival research.

47 For a discussion of this point, see my 'The Centre Will Not Hold: On Changing Principles of Political Hope', *Soundings* 60: 2015.

48 The basis of Rzewski's work is the song of the same title by Sergio Ortega.

49 Covent Garden in the centre of London housed a large fruit and vegetable market that was scheduled for demolition in 1968. The area held a large and long-established working-class community who launched a campaign to prevent the market site being demolished and replaced by a hotel, conference and office complex. The plans were overturned after a public enquiry, leading to the transformation of the surrounding warehouses and the market itself into boutique shopping and workshops for creative industry.

50 See Joseph Schumpeter, *Capitalism, Socialism and Democracy* (1942). See also Paul Mason, *Postcapitalism* (2015), for a good discussion of Schumpeter's view of capitalism as a simultaneously creative and destructive force.

51 For a detailed discussion of the role of the archive and memory politics in the transition from Communism in the Eastern Bloc countries, see Michael Bernhard and Jan Kubik, *Twenty Years after Communism: The Politics of Memory and Commemoration* (2014).

52 Mikhail Bakhtin, *The Dialogic Imagination: Four Essays* (1982).

53 See Frédéric Rouvillois, *L'Invention du progrès: aux origines de la pensée totalitaire* (1996).

54 For a good summary of debates around adoption, see Peter J. Conn, *Adoption: A Brief Social and Cultural History* (2013); and Ivor Gaber and Janed Aldridge, eds., *In the Best Interests of the Child: Culture, Identity and Transracial Adoption* (1994). For a Foucauldian interpretation of this history, see Sally Sales, *Adoption, Family and the Paradox of Origins* (2012).

55 For a philosophical discussion of adoption identity politics, see Denise Riley, *The Words of Selves: Identity, Solidarity, Irony* (1988).

56 Freud's theory of the family romance (1908), as a myth of origins, postulates that children phantasise they are adopted by projecting an idealised version of their birth parents onto exotic strangers in order to protect its early narcissistic identifications with them. For a recent summary of this theory, see Josie Oppenheim, 'The Magic of Adoption: The Pre-Oedipal Genesis of the Family Romance', *Modern Psychoanalysis* 34 (1): 2009. Note that the word 'phantasy', distinct from 'fantasy', refers to the language of the unconscious found in dreams and in what has been termed 'magical thinking' or 'primary process thinking'.

57 For a critique of contemporary futurology, see John Urry, *What Is the Future* (2016). For an attempt to construct a Left futurology, see Nick Srnicek and Alex Williams, *Inventing the Future* (2016). For a critique of what is sometimes called 'accelerationism', see Benjamin Noys, *Malign Velocities* (2013).

58 The chrono-topographic concept of proto- and retro-modernism proposed in what follows attempts to break with the linear narrative of 'modernisation'. Most accounts continue to operate with a simple scheme of modernity in which this is identified by a number of structural features whose absence is then used to define its pre- and postmodern forms. In order to apply an empirical principle of periodisation to this scheme, modernity is then often

equated with industrialisation so that the preindustrial is made to correspond to the premodern, Fordism or mass production is associated with high modernity and the postindustrial with postmodernism. There is no denying that there are some important links, especially between the postindustrial and the postmodern, given the growth of creative industries and capitalism's cultural turn. Nevertheless a model which assumes such a tight fit between cultural and economic forms is as implausible as one which asserts that there is an inevitable lag between them with culture always anticipating or playing catch-up to the economic. Bruno Latour, in his appropriately titled *We Have Never Been Modern* (1996), demolished the Marxist base/superstructure model by demonstrating that the implied relations of correspondence are always in process of transformation, or rather transubstantiation: what is 'base' at one moment is 'superstructure' at another, and vice versa. 'Modernity' is simply the name we have learnt to give to this process.

59   The classic discussion of nostalgia and kitsch is Fred Davis, *Yearning for Yesterday: A Sociology of Nostalgia* (1979). See also Alastair Bonnett, *The Geography of Nostalgia*.

60   Ernst Bloch, *The Principle of Hope* (1995).

61   See Orhan Pamuk, *The Innocence of Objects* (2012) and *Istanbul: Memories and the City* (2004).

62   Walter Benjamin, 'Theses on the Philosophy of History', in *Illuminations* (1965 [1940]).

63   See the discussion by Svetlana Alexievich in the introduction to her *Secondhand Time: The Last of the Soviets* (2017).

64   See Leo Braudy, *The Frenzy of Renown* (1986) for a historical analysis of changing forms of fame.

65   For an analysis of contemporary trends in memoir writing, see my 'Recognizing in the Inferno That Which Is Not: Reflections on Memoir Writing'. *History Workshop Journal* 74 (1): 2012.

66   Max Weber, *The Theory of Social and Economic Organization*, ed. Talcott Parsons (1947).

67   See Aaron Jaffe and Jonathan Goldman, eds., *Modernist Star Maps: Celebrity, Modernity, Culture* (2010); and P. David Marshall, ed., *The Celebrity Culture Reader* (2005).

68   See Martijn Konings, *The Emotional Logic of Capitalism: What Progressives Have Missed* (2015).

69   See Jonathan Crary, *Suspensions of Perception: Attention, Spectacle and Modern Culture* (2000).

70   A good example of this is the so-called 'Bowie bond' which refers to the practice, inaugurated by David Bowie's financial advisors, of raising a large loan against future royalties in return for a high rate of annual interest over an extended period. The commercialisation of future cultural assets has led to ever-closer integration between financial services and the creative industries, expanding the role of what Marx called 'fictitious capital' into areas hitherto the preserve of living labour.

71   The MetaArchive Cooperative is an international digital preservation network composed of libraries, archives, and other digital memory institutions founded in 2004 with the mission of fostering better understanding of distributed digital preservation methods and creating stable, geographically dispersed 'dark archives' of digital content. A dark archive is one used for preservation rather than public access. The MetaArchive preserves a wide variety of data types, including electronic theses and dissertations, digital newspapers, archival content such as photograph collections and A/V materials, business/e-records, and datasets. See https://metaarchive.org.

72   Jorge Luis Borges, 'The Library of Babel' (1941). Recently an attempt has been made to apply Borgesian principles to the creation of a digital library which would contain texts with every possible combination of words. Libraryofbabel. info currently allows users to choose from about 10^{4677} potential books. The site also features a search tool which allows users to retrieve the location in the library of any known page of text. Yet its creator Jonathan Basile ruefully notes that 'after searching through endless books, both in the process of testing the site and because I myself cannot shake the compulsion it produces, the longest legible title I have found is Dog'.

73   See Rebecca Lossin, 'Against the Universal Library' in *New Left Review* 107 (2017) and the study by Nicholson Baker, *Double Fold: Libraries and the Assault on Paper* (2002).

74   See, for example, the discussion of Instagram and Facebook in Deborah Lupton, *The Quantified Self* (2017).

75   François Schuiten and Benoît Peeters, *L'Archiviste* (1987).

76   Alexander Pope, *The House of Fame* (1715).

77   See Bridget Fowler, *The Obituary as Collective Memory* (2007).

78   'New Times' was a banner under which the democratic Left in Britain regrouped in response to Tony Blair's version of a 'third way' between state socialism and free-market capitalism. It was a loose-knit alliance centred on the journals *New Socialist* and *Marxism Today*, informed by cultural and identity politics and by a desire to reject the ideological baggage of both Labourism and old-style Marxism/Leninism. See the book by two of its leading thinkers, Stuart Hall and Martin Jacques, *New Times: The Changing Face of Politics in the 1990s* (1990).

79   See Zygmunt Bauman, *Mortality, Immortality and Other Life Strategies* (1992).

80   James Agee and Walker Evans, *Let Us Now Praise Famous Men* (1969).

81   See George Marcus, 'The Once and Future Ethnographic Archive' (1998).

82   This distinction was first drawn by Robert Putnam in *Bowling Alone* (2000) and refers to two different forms of social capital, one based on closed and the other on open or distributed networks. Here I am applying the distinction to cultural capital as defined by Pierre Bourdieu, in 'Forms of Capital' (1986), in terms of a threefold typology: (a) embodied in dispositions of mind and body associated with 'taste'; (b) objectified in cultural goods and artefacts; and (c) institutionalised in forms of cultural or educational dis/qualification. Though useful as an analytic tool, Bourdieu's scheme does not in itself help us to understand articulations between the three types within concrete cultural

forms, which are almost always hybrids. The archive, for example, involves all three types of cultural capital but cannot be reduced to any of them.

83 In *Personal Knowledge: Towards a Post-Critical Philosophy* (2002), Michael Polanyi distinguishes between two generic types of knowledge: the first (tacit) is centred on practical sensuous activity and on 'know-how' requiring no explicit theorisation to be performed, while the second (coded) consists of reflexive methodological rules for staking knowledge claims in a particular domain of its application. This distinction was used in Basil Bernstein's *Class, Codes and Control* (1985) for his model of restricted and elaborated socio-linguistic codes. Bernstein later developed this model into a broader picture of the pedagogic transmission of cultural capital centred on the concepts of the classification and framing of knowledge.

84 The distinction was first made by the Russian formalists Vladimir Propp (1968) and Viktor Shklovsky (1965) to distinguish between the raw material of a story evidenced by the chronology of events (*fabula*) and its narrative organisation or plot (*syuzhet*). Critics such as Bakhtin and Derrida have objected to the primacy the Formalists have given to plot, insisting that the unfolding of a sequence of events has its own irreducible dynamic. I have followed Tristan Todorov's (1990) reformulation of this distinction into two complementary modes of archival discourse.

85 Indeed the term was originally applied to a bitter debate over Freud's legacy, in particular his concept of 'false memory' in cases of child abuse, between defenders of his theory of childhood Oedipal trauma and its unconscious repression and feminists involved in the recovered-memory movement who argued that the account of abuse by victims should be treated as a social fact, unless proved otherwise, and not a sexual phantasy. See Frederick Crews et al., *The Memory Wars: Freud's Legacy in Dispute* (1995).

86 See the contributions to Kwesi Owusu (ed.) *Black British Culture and Society* (1999).

87 See Arjun Appadurai, 'Archive and Aspiration' in Joke Brouwer and Arjen Mulder (eds.) *Information Is Alive* (2003).

88 For what follows I am indebted to the volunteer staff and to the article by Rhiannon Firth, 'Critical Cartography as Anarchist Pedagogy: Ideas for Praxis Inspired by the Info 56a Map Archive', *Interface* 16 (1): 2014.

89 *Freedom* was founded in 1886 by Peter Kropotkin and others as the weekly newspaper of the anarchist movement in Britain and appeared regularly until 2014, when it was converted to a monthly magazine. It is still published by Freedom Press, based in Whitechapel.

90 See Walter Benjamin, *Illuminations* (1978), p. 67

91 C. Wright Mills, *The Sociological Imagination* (1999).

92 For an interesting analysis which attempts to build epistemological bridges between historical materialism and complexity theory, see Luca Basso, *Marx and Singularity: From the Early Writings to the Grundrisse* (2012).

93 David Graeber, *Possibilities: Essays on Hierarchy, Rebellion, and Desire* (2007).

94 Jay Winter, *Sites of Memory, Sites of Mourning: The Great War in European Cultural History* (2014).

95 The survey was carried out between 15 November and 3 December 2014. The findings will be discussed in a forthcoming paper, 'A Time to Remember', which will appear first on my website: http//www.philcohenworks.com.

96 David Rieff, *In Praise of Forgetting: Historical Memory and Its Ironies* (2016). For a contrary view which nevertheless shares some common ground regarding the culture of amnesia, see Harald Weinrich, *Lethe: The Art and Critique of Forgetting* (2004).

97 In *The Hidden Injuries of Class* (1977) Richard Sennett anticipates Bourdieu's theory of symbolic violence in focussing on the way patterns of class discrimination and domination are internalised by those subjected to them, for example in the form of low self-esteem, lack of self-respect or identification with the dominant culture.

98 For a discussion of contemporary class identity politics in Britain, see my 'Finding Uncommon ground: Working Class Identity Politics after Labourism', *Soundings* 66: 2017. For an interesting comparison between the British and American situation, see Justin Gest, *The New Minority: White Working Class Politics in an Age of Immigration and Inequality* (2017).

99 See http://glcstory.co.uk for further information about this initiative. For an attempt to resurrect this form of radical municipal socialism, see Ken Livingstone, *Being Red: A Politics for the Future* (2016).

100 See Raoul Vaneigem, *The Revolution of Everyday Life* (2012 [1967]) and Roberto Unger, *The Left Alternative* (2009).

101 See Mieke Bal, *Travelling Concepts in the Humanities: A Rough Guide* (2002) and Marilyn Strathern, *Commons and Borderlands: Working Papers on Interdisciplinarity, Accountability and the Flow of Knowledge* (2004).

102 See Bruno Latour, *Reassembling the Social: An Introduction to Actor-Network Theory* (2005).

103 This is the main aim of the MayDay Rooms, although they have not so far used participatory action research (PAR) for this purpose. The Livingmaps Network is currently developing a Citizen's Atlas of London through the use of participatory mapping in community workshops in areas of the city threatened with major regeneration and gentrification. For further information, see www.livingmaps.org.uk.

104 This Brooklyn-based archive focussing on the relationship between cultural production and social movements has developed a critical and participatory pedagogy using its collection of political ephemera to explore the rich material history of radical protest. See www.interferencearchive.org.

105 This strategy, purpose-built for the hermeneutic archive, has been developed most fully by Carlo Ginzburg in *Threads and Traces: True, False, Fiction* (2012) and in *Clues, Myths and the Historical Method* (1989). It is also mandated by Wolfgang Ernst's vision of the digital archive as a new kind of research engine: see his *Digital Memory and the Archive* (2013).

106 See Hans Ulrich Obrist, *Ways of Curating* (2014); and, for a critical view, see David Balzer, *Curationism: How Curating Took Over the Art World and Everything Else* (2014); a good analysis of current trends is Andreas Huyssen, *Twilight Memories: Making Time in a Culture of Amnesia* (1995)

107 The term 'roots radical' was initially used to self-describe a politicised off-shoot of reggae and was popularised in eponymous songs by Jimmy Cliff and Desmond Dekker. Punk bands Stiff Little Fingers and Rancid also took up the theme. The genealogical focus on tracing ethnic origins as an exploration of a lost cultural heritage predated its musical expression and was given a strong afrocentric twist with the publication of Alex Haley's 1976 novel *Roots: The Saga of an American Family*, which became the basis for a famous TV series. There was a parallel emergence of roots radical historiography, tunnelling back into the past to find evidence of minority ethnic achievement and struggle marginalised or ignored in the accounts of the dominant society. The methodology of these projects involved joining up the dots into a linear narrative of an enduring presence and has been criticised for its tunnel vision. As an archival strategy it has been an important strand in populist versions of black history in both Britain and the USA.

108 Hal Foster, 'An Archival Impulse', *October* 110: 2004.

109 See Deborah Lupton, *The Quantified Self* (2016).

110 For a discussion of citizen social science and participatory action research, see my article 'Our Kind of Town: Citizen Social Science, Participatory Mapping and the Struggle for a Just City' in *Livingmaps Review* nos. 1 and 2, at www.livingmaps.review.

111 See Dorothy Sheridan and Angus Calder, *Speak for Yourself: A Mass Observation Anthology* (1984); and Dorothy Sheridan and Brian Street, *Writing Ourselves* (2000).

112 See Carolyn Steedman, 'Something She Called a Fever: Michelet, Derrida, and Dust', *American Historical Review* 106 (4): 2001; Arlette Farge, *The Allure of the Archives* (2013 [1989]); and Rebecca Lossin, 'Against the Universal Library', *New Left Review* 107: 2017.

113 'Tamar Garb in Conversation with Christian Boltanski', in Didier Semin et al., *Christian Boltanski* (2001).

114 See Christian Boltanski, *The Possible Life of Christian Boltanski* (2009).

115 Quoted in Juliet Bingham, ed., *Ilya and Emilia Kabakov: Not Everyone Will Be Taken into the Future* (2017).

116 Quoted in *Not Everyone Will Be Taken into the Future*. For a discussion of this work, see the essay by Kate Fowle in this catalogue.

117 The lived memory of this transitional period is documented to brilliant effect by Svetlana Alexievich in *Secondhand Time: The Last of the Soviets* (2017).

118 See in particular Alessandro Portelli, *The Death of Luigi Trastulli and Other Stories* (1991) and *The Battle of Valle Giulia: Oral History and the Art of Dialogue* (1997).

119 Studs Terkel was blacklisted by McCarthy and investigated for over forty-five years by the FBI for Communist sympathies. He was at the very least a fellow-traveller. It is worth noting that many currently acclaimed people in the US were more-or-less Communists but have had that fact completely erased from their public biographies. I am grateful to Donald Nicholson-Smith for drawing this to my attention.

120 See Studs Terkel, *Hope Dies Last: Making a Difference in an Indifferent World* (2005).

121 This territory is explored in Alain Resnais's famous film about the Bibliothèque Nationale in Paris, *Toute la Mémoire du Monde* (1956). Resnais portrays the archive as a fortress or prison of Reason in which knowledge is locked away but subject to entropy. It is as if the very materiality of the building and the documents it houses defies conscious organisation and make its content subject to the second law of thermodynamics. See Uriel Orlow, 'Latent Archives, Roving Lens' in *Ghosting: The Role of the Archive within Contemporary Artists* Film and Video, eds. Jane Connarty and Josephine Lanyon (2006).

122 See Arlette Farge, *The Allure of the Archives* (2013)

123 Italo Calvino, *Invisible Cities* (1997).

124 Helene Demuth is also buried in the Marx family grave alongside Jenny. Helene was for many years housekeeper to the Marx family, becoming Karl's lifelong friend, political confidant and, it is widely believed, eventually a lover. She gave birth to his child in 1851, fatherhood being claimed by Engels to save the Marxes' marriage. The baby was placed with working-class foster parents in London, where he became a toolmaker and grew into a lonely and embittered man, shunned by both his real and adoptive fathers and written out of the family history. Needless to say, *this* history, which has so much to tell us about Victorian bourgeois domestic life and its cruel moral hypocrisies, has been almost totally ignored by Marx's later biographers. See Ralph Buultjens, *The Secret Life of Karl Marx* (1987) and Mary Gabriel, *Love and Capital: Karl and Jenny Marx and the Birth of Revolution* (2011).

125 For a discussion of the 'island story' and its contemporary deployment, see Chapter 8 of Phil Cohen *On the Wrong Side of the Track* (2013).

126 For an interesting, if somewhat superficial, comparative study of white working-class culture and its relation to right-wing populism in the American and British context, see Justin Gest, *The New Minority: White Working Class Politics in an Age of Immigration and Inequality* (2017).

Further Reading

The following texts were consulted and/or referenced in the course of writing this one. They have been organised into eight themes for readers who may be interested in following up some of these ideas. I have marked books of especial use or interest with an asterisk. Please note that I have included here some texts that are not referenced in the endnotes because they are of general interest and important for the development of the argument.

The Archive as Model and Metaphor

Theodor Adorno. *Minima Moralia: Reflections from Damaged Life*. London: Verso, 2010.

*Arjun Appadurai. 'Archive and Aspiration' in J. Brouwer and A. Mulder (eds.), *Information Is Alive*. Rotterdam: V2/NAI, 2003.

Aleida Asman. 'Canon and Archive' in Jeffrey Olick, Vered Vinitzky-Seroussi, and Daniel Levy (eds.), *The Collective Memory Reader*. Oxford: Oxford University Press, 2011.

*Walter Benjamin. *The Arcades Project*. Cambridge, MA: Harvard University Press, 1999.

Basil Bernstein. *Class, Codes and Control, Vol. 1*. London: Routledge, 1985.

Frances Blouin and William Rosenberg. *Archives, Documentation and the Institutions of Social Memory*. Ann Arbor: University of Michigan Press, 2006.

Luc Boltanski and Laurent Thévenot. *On Justification: Economies of Worth*. Princeton: Princeton University Press, 2006.

Pierre Bourdieu. 'Forms of Capital' in John G. Richardson (ed.), *Handbook of Theory and Research in the Sociology of Education*. New York: Greenwood 1986.

Harriet Bradley. 'The Seductions of the Archive'. *History of the Human Sciences* 12 (2): 1999.

*Jens Brockmeier. *Beyond the Archive: Memory, Narrative, and the Autobiographical Process*. Oxford: Oxford University Press, 2015.

Jacques Derrida. *Dissemination*. Chicago: University of Chicago Press, 1981.

*Jacques Derrida. *Archive Fever: A Freudian Impression.* Chicago: University of Chicago Press, 1996.

*Wolfgang Ernst. *Digital Memory and the Archive.* Minneapolis: University of Minnesota Press, 2013.

*Arlette Farge. *The Allure of the Archives.* New Haven, CT: Yale University Press, 2013.

Michel Foucault. *The Archaeology of Knowledge.* London: Routledge, 1989.

Jacques Le Goff and Pierre Nora (eds.). *Constructing the Past: Essays in Historical Methodology.* Cambridge: Cambridge University Press, 1985.

Jacques Le Goff. *History and Memory.* New York: Columbia University Press, 1992.

Stuart Hall. 'Constructing an Archive'. *Third Text* 15 (54): 2001.

Carolyn Hamilton et al. (eds.). *Refiguring the Archive.* Dordrecht: Kluwder Academic, 2013.

Albert Khan. *Archives of the Planet.* www.collections.albert-khan.albert-khan.haute-de-seine.fr

Bruno Latour. *Reassembling the Social: An Introduction to Actor-Network Theory.* Oxford: Oxford University Press, 2005.

Michael Lynch. 'Archives in Formation'. *History of the Human Sciences* 12 (2): 1999.

Marlene Manoff. 'Theories of the Archive'. *Libraries and the Academy* 4 (1): 2004.

George Marcus. 'The Once and Future Ethnographic Archive'. *History of the Human Sciences* 11 (4): 1998.

*Charles Merewether (ed.). *The Archive.* Cambridge, MA: MIT Press, 2006.

Patrick Modiano. *The Search Warrant.* London: Harvill, 2000.

Philip Monk. *Disassembling the Archive: Fiona Tan.* Toronto: Art Gallery of York University 2007.

Hans Ulrich Obrist. *Ways of Curating.* London: Allen Lane 2014.

Michael Polanyi. *Personal Knowledge: Towards a Post-Critical Philosophy.* London: Routledge, 1962.

Paul Ricoeur. *Time and Narrative,* Vol. 3. Chicago: University of Chicago Press, 1988.

Allan Sekula. 'The Body and the Archive'. *October* 39: 1986.

Carolyn Steedman. 'Something She Called a Fever: Michelet, Derrida, and Dust'. *American Historical Review* 106 (4): 2001.

Tzvetan Todorov. *Genres in Discourse.* Cambridge: Cambridge University Press, 1990.

James V. Wertsch. 'Beyond the Archival Model of Memory and the Affordances and Constraints of Narrative'. *Culture & Psychology* 17: 2011.

Paul Voss and Marta Werner. 'Towards a Poetics of the Archive'. *Studies in the Literary Imagination* 32 (1): 1999.

Counter Culture

Tariq Ali. *Street Fighting Years: An Autobiography of the Sixties.* London: Verso 2005.

Ron Bailey. *The Squatters.* Harmondsworth: Penguin, 1973.

Paul Berman. *A Tale of Two Utopias: The Political Journey of the Generation of 1968.* W.W. Norton, 1996.

Victoria Broackes and Geoffrey Marsh (eds.). *You Say You Want a Revolution: Records and Rebels 1966–1970.* London: Victoria and Albert Museum, 2016.

Phil Cohen. *Reading Room Only: Memoir of a Radical Bibliophile.* Nottingham: Five Leaves, 2013.

Phil Cohen. *Rethinking the Youth Question*. London: Palgrave Macmillan, 1997.

*Thomas Frank. *Conquest of the Cool: Business Culture, Counter Culture and the Rise of Hip Consumerism*. Chicago: University of Chicago Press, 1997.

Hywel Francis. *History on Our Side: Wales and the 1984–85 Miners' Strike*. London: Lawrence and Wishart, 2015.

Ronald Fraser. *1968: A Student Generation in Revolt*. London: Chatto and Windus, 1988.

Samuel Fuller. *144 Piccadilly*. London: New English Library, 1969.

Todd Gitlin. *The Sixties: Years of Hope, Days of Rage*. New York: Random House, 1993.

George Melly. *Revolt into Style: The Pop Arts*. Oxford: Oxford University Press, 1989.

Barry Miles. *1969*. London: Pimlico, 2003.

Robin Morgan and Ariel Leve. *1963: The Year of the Revolution, How Youth Changed the World with Music Arts and Fashion*. New York: It Books, 2013.

Frank Mort. *Capital Affairs: London and the Making of the Permissive Society*. New Haven, CT: Yale University Press, 2010.

Jeff Nuttall. *Bomb Culture*. London: Paladin, 1970.

Kwesi Owusu (ed.). *Black British Culture and Society*. London: Routledge, 2006.

*Luisa Passerini. *Autobiography of a Generation: Italy 1968*. Hanover, NH: University Press of New England, 1996.

*Dick Pountain and Dave Robins. *Cool Rules: Anatomy of an Attitude*. London: Reaktion Books, 2000.

Charles Radcliffe. *Don't Start Me Talkin'*. 2 Vols. London: King Mob, 2015.

*Kristin Ross. *May '68 and Its Afterlives*. Chicago: University of Chicago Press, 2002.

Theodor Roszak. *The Making of a Counter Culture*. Berkeley: University of California Press, 1995.

Jon Savage. *1966: The Year the Decade Exploded*. London: Faber & Faber, 2015.

*Alexander Vasudevan. *The Autonomous City: A History of Urban Squatting*. Oxford: Oxford University Press, 2017.

Aro Velmet. '40 Years Is Enough: Myth and Memory in French Commemorations of May 1968'. Penn Humanities Forum on Connections. 2010.

Left Legacies and the Dialectic of Generations

*Luc Boltanski and Eve Chiapello. *The New Spirit of Capitalism*. London: Verso, 2007.

Brian Cathcart. *The Case of Stephen Lawrence*. Harmondsworth: Penguin 2000.

John Carey. *The Intellectuals and the Masses: Pride and Prejudice in the Literary Intelligentsia, 1880–1939*. Chicago: Academy Chicago Publishers, 2000.

T.J. Clark. 'For a Left with No Future'. *New Left Review* 74: 2012.

Phil Cohen. 'Finding Uncommon Ground: Working-Class Identity Politics after Labourism'. *Soundings* 66: 2017.

Michael Collins. *The Likes of Us: A Biography of the White Working Class*. London: Granta 2006.

Stuart Hall and Martin Jacques. *New Times: The Changing Face of Politics in the 1990s*. London: Lawrence and Wishart, 1990.

Ken Livingstone. *Being Red: A Politics for the Future*. Pluto Press, 2016.

Fredric Jameson. *Valences of the Dialectic*. London: Verso, 2009.

Owen Jones. *Chavs: The Demonization of the Working Class*. London: Verso, 2011.

Linda Macdowell. *Redundant Masculinities? Employment Change and White Working Class Youth*. Oxford: Blackwell, 2003.

*Karl Mannheim. 'The Problem of Generations' in *Essays in the Sociology of Knowledge*. London: Routledge, 1997.

Karl Marx and Friedrich Engels. *The German Ideology*. London: Lawrence and Wishart, 1970.

Karl Marx. *The 18th Brumaire of Louis Napoleon*. London: Lawrence and Wishart, 1972.

Barbara Myerhoff. *Remembered Lives: The Work of Ritual, Story Telling and Growing Older*. Ann Arbor: University of Michigan Press, 1992.

Alexander Mitscherlich. *Society without the Father*. London: Tavistock Publications, 1969.

Michael Mitterauer. *History of Youth*. London: Blackwell, 1992.

Denis O'Hearn. *Bobby Sands: Nothing but an Unfinished Song*. London: Pluto Press, 2016.

Robert Putnam. *Bowling Alone: The Collapse and Revival of American Community*. New York: Simon and Schuster, 2000.

Jonathon Rose. *The Intellectual Life of the British Working Classes*. Oxford: Oxford University Press, 2001.

Dorothy Sheridan. *Speak for Yourself: A Mass-Observation Anthology*. London: Cape, 1984.

Richard Sennett and Jonathon Cobb. *The Hidden Injuries of Class*. Cambridge: Cambridge University Press, 1974.

Guy Standing. *The Precariat: The New Dangerous Class*. London: Bloomsbury Academic, 2011.

Ruy Teixeira and Joel Rogers. *America's Forgotten Majority: Why the White Working Class Still Matters*. New York: Basic Books, 2001.

The Chronotopes of Modernity

Arjun Appadurai. *The Future as a Cultural Fact: Essays on the Global Condition*. London: Verso, 2010.

Mikhail Bakhtin. *The Dialogic Imagination: Four Essays*. Austin: University of Texas Press, 1982.

Marshall Berman. *All That Is Solid Melts into Air: The Experience of Modernity*. London: Verso, 2010.

Alastair Bonnett. *Geography of Nostalgia: Local and Global Perspectives on Modernity and Loss*. London: Routledge, 2016.

Fred Davis. *Yearning for Yesterday: A Sociology of Nostalgia*. London: Collier Macmillan, 1979.

Guy Debord. *Society of the Spectacle*. New York: Zone Books, 1994.

Johannes Fabian. *Time and the Other: How Anthropology Makes Its Object*. New York: Columbia University Press, 2002.

Alfred Gell. *The Anthropology of Time: Cultural Construction of Temporal Maps and Images*. Oxford: Berg, 1992.

Eric Hobsbawm and Terence Ranger (eds.). *The Invention of Tradition*. Cambridge: Cambridge University Press, 1992.

Martijn Konings. *The Emotional Logic of Capitalism: What Progressives Have Missed.* Stanford, CA: Stanford University Press, 2015.

Bruno Latour. *We Have Never Been Modern.* Cambridge: Cambridge University Press, 1996.

Andrew McCullogh. *Charisma and Patronage: Reasoning with Max Weber.* London: Routledge, 2016.

Orhan Pamuk. *The Innocence of Objects: The Museum of Innocence.* New York: Abrams, 2012.

Orhan Pamuk. *Istanbul: Memories and the City.* New York: Vintage International, 2004.

Frederic Rouvillois. *L'Invention du progrès: aux origines de la pensée totalitaire.* Paris: Klime, 1996.

François Schuiten and Benoît Peeters. *L'Archiviste.* Brussels: Casterman, 1987.

Raphael Samuels. *Theatres of Memory: Past and Present in Contemporary Culture.* London: Verso, 2012.

*Carl Schorske. *Thinking with History: Explorations in the Passage to Modernity.* Princeton, NJ: Princeton University Press, 1996.

Bill Schwarz. 'Memory, Temporality, Modernity: Les lieux de mémoire' in Sussanah Radstone and Bill Schwarz (eds.), *Memory: History, Theories, Debates.* New York: Fordham University Press, 2010.

Richard Terdiman. *Present Past: Modernity and the Memory Crisis.* New York: Cornell University Press, 1993.

Hayden White. *Metahistory: The Historical Imagination in Nineteenth-Century Europe.* Baltimore: Johns Hopkins Press, 1973.

Paul Virno. *Déjà Vu and the End of History.* London: Verso, 2015.

Paul Thompson. *Voice of the Past: Oral History.* Oxford: Oxford University Press, 2000.

Memory Politics

Giorgio Agamben. *Remnants of Auschwitz: The Witness and the Archive.* New York: Zone Books, 1999.

Ulrich Baer. *Spectral Evidence: The Photography of Trauma.* Cambridge, MA: MIT Press, 2002.

*Lauren Berlant. *Cruel Optimism.* Durham, NC: Duke University Press, 2011.

Michael Bernhard and Jan Kubik. *Twenty Years after Communism: The Politics of Memory and Commemoration.* New York: Oxford University Press, 2014.

Christian Boltanski. *Reconstitution.* London: Whitechapel Art Gallery, 1990.

M. Christine Boyer. *The City of Collective Memory.* Cambridge, MA: MIT Press, 1994.

Judith Butler. *Precarious Life: The Powers of Mourning and Violence.* London: Verso, 2004.

Sue Campbell. *Our Faithfulness to the Past: The Ethics and Politics of Memory.* New York: Oxford University Press, 2014.

Ian Cobain. *The History Thieves: Secrecy, Lies and the Shaping of a Modern Nation.* London: Portobello Press, 2016.

Phil Cohen. 'Recognizing in the Inferno That Which Is Not: Reflections on Memoir Writing'. *History Workshop Journal* 74 (1): 2012.

Alan Confino. 'Collective Memory and Cultural History'. *American Historical Review* 102 (5): 1997.

Frederick Crews et al. *The Memory Wars: Freud's Legacy in Dispute.* New York: New York Review of Books, 1995.

*David L. Eng and David Kazanjian (eds.). *Loss: The Politics of Mourning.* Berkeley: University of California Press, 2002.

Ian Farr (ed.). *Memory.* Documents in Contemporary Art. Cambridge, MA: MIT Press, 2012.

Kenneth E. Foote. 'To Remember and Forget: Archive, Memory, and Culture'. *American Archivist* 53 (3): 1990.

Sigmund Freud. *On Murder, Mourning and Melancholia.* New York: Penguin, 2005.

Leticia Glocer Fiorini, Thierry Bokanowski, and Sergio Lewkowicz (eds.). *On Freud's 'Mourning and Melancholia'.* London: International Psychoanalytic Association, 2007.

Ian Hacking. *Rewriting the Soul: Multiple Personality and the Sciences of Memory.* Princeton, NJ: Princeton University Press, 2001.

Frigga Haug. 'Memory Work'. *Australian Feminist Studies* 23 (58): 2008.

Marianne Hirsch. *The Generation of Postmemory: Writing and Visual Culture after the Holocaust.* New York: Columbia University Press, 2012.

*Andreas Huyssen. *Twilight Memories: Marking Time in a Culture of Amnesia.* New York: Routledge, 1995.

Meg Jensen. 'Post-traumatic Memory Projects: Autobiographical Fiction and Counter-monuments'. *Textual Practice* 28 (4): 2014.

Milan Kundera. *The Book of Laughter and Forgetting.* Harmondsworth: Penguin, 1981.

Hilda Kean. 'Whose Archive? Whose History? Destruction of Archives at Ruskin College, Oxford'. History Workshop. www.historyworkshop.org.uk/whose-archive-whose-history-destruction-of-archives-at-ruskin-college-oxford/.

John Lennon and Malcolm Foley. *Dark Tourism.* London: Continuum, 2000.

Jean-Philippe Mathy. *Melancholy Politics: Loss, Mourning and Memory in Late Modern France.* University Park: Pennsylvania State University Press, 2011.

Jeffrey Olick, Vered Vinitzky-Seroussi, and Daniel Levy (eds.). *The Collective Memory Reader.* Oxford: Oxford University Press, 2011.

Luisa Passerini. *Memory and Utopia: The Primacy of Inter-Subjectivity.* London: Equina, 2007.

Susannah Radstone and Bill Schwarz (eds.). *Memory: Histories, Theories, Debates.* New York: Fordham University Press, 2010.

Thomas Richards. The Imperial Archive: Knowledge and Fantasy of Empire. London: Verso 1993.

*David Rieff. *In Praise of Forgetting: Historical Memory and Its Ironies.* London: Faber, 2016.

*Ann Laura Stoler. *Along the Archival Grain: Epistemic Anxieties and Colonial Common Sense.* Princeton, NJ: Princeton University Press 2009.

Marita Sturken. *Tourists of History.* London: Routledge, 2015.

Tzvetan Todorov. *Hope and Memory: Reflections on the 20th Century.* London: Atlantic Books, 2005.

Harald Weinrich. *Lethe: The Art and Critique of Forgetting.* Ithaca, NY: Cornell University Press, 2004.

Jay Winter. *Sites of Memory, Sites of Mourning: The Great War in European Cultural History*. Cambridge, MA: Cambridge University Press, 2014.

James E. Young. *The Texture of Memory: Holocaust Memorials and Meaning*. New Haven, CT: Yale University Press, 1993.

David Zeitlyn. 'Anthropology in Aid of the Archives: Possible Futures and Contingent Pasts'. *American Anthropology* 24 (1): 2012.

Fame, Heritage and the Technologies of Immortality

James Agee and Walker Evans. *Let Us Now Praise Famous Men*. London: Panther Books, 1969.

*Zygmunt Bauman. *Mortality, Immortality and Other Life Strategies*. Cambridge: Polity Press, 1992.

*Leo Braudy. *The Frenzy of Renown: Fame and Its History*. Oxford: Oxford University Press, 1986.

James Brook and Iain A. Boal. *Resisting the Virtual Life: The Culture and Politics of Information*. San Francisco: City Lights Press, 1995.

W.H. Chou. 'Media Mediocracy': Live Archiving as an Intervention in Preserving Cultural Heritage'. *International Journal of Arts and Technology* 8 (1): 2010.

Jonathan Crary. *Suspensions of Perception: Attention, Spectacle, and Modern Culture*. Cambridge, MA: MIT Press, 2000.

Régis Debray. *Media Manifestos: On the Technological Transmission of Cultural Forms*. London: Verso, 1996.

Bridget Fowler. *The Obituary as Collective Memory*. London: Routledge, 2007.

Aaron Jaffe and Jonathan Goldman. *Modernist Star Maps: Celebrity, Modernity, Culture*. Farnham: Ashgate, 2010.

Philip Hardie. *Rumour and Renown: Representations of Fama in Western Literature*. Cambridge: Cambridge University Press, 2012.

Thomas Laqueur. *The Work of the Dead: A Cultural History of Mortal Remains*. Princeton, NJ: University Press, 2015.

P. David Marshall (ed.). *The Celebrity Culture Reader*. London: Routledge, 2006.

Edgar Morin. *The Stars*. Minneapolis: University of Minnesota Press, 2005.

David Park (ed.). *The Long History of New Media: Technology, Historiography, and Contextualising Newness*. New York: Peter Lang, 2011.

Alexander Pope. *The Temple of Fame*. 1715.

Bernard Stiegler. *For a New Critique of Political Economy*. Cambridge: Polity, 2013.

E.P. Thompson. 'The Grid of Inheritance' in Jack Goody, Joan Thirsk, and E.P. Thompson (eds.), *Family and Inheritance: Rural Society in Western Europe*. Cambridge: Cambridge University Press, 1976.

The Living Anarchive

*Svetlana Aleksievich. *Second-Hand Time: The Last of the Soviets*. London: Bantam Press, 2017.

Mieke Bal. *Travelling Concepts in the Humanities: A Rough Guide*. Toronto: University of Toronto Press, 2002.

Luca Basso. *Marx and Singularity: From the Early Writings to the Grundrisse*. Leiden: Brill, 2012.

Juliet Bingham, Ilya Kabakov, and Emilia Kabakov (eds.). *Not Everyone Will Be Taken into the Future*. London: Tate Publishing, 2017.

Ernst Bloch. *The Principle of Hope*. Cambridge, MA: MIT Press, 1995.

Christian Boltanski. *The Possible Life of Christian Boltanski*. London: Whitechapel Gallery, 2009.

Gundhild Borggreen and Rune Gade. *Performing Archive/Archives of Performance*. University of Copenhagen, 2008.

Phil Cohen. 'The Centre Will Not Hold: On Changing Principles of Political Hope'. *Soundings* 60: 2015.

Jane Connarty and Josephine Lanyon. *Ghosting: The Role of the Archive in Contemporary Film and Video*. Bristol: Picture This, 2006.

Vincent Crapanzano. *Imaginative Horizons: An Essay in Literary-Philosophical Anthropology*. Chicago: University of Chicago Press, 2004.

Hal Foster. 'An Archival Impulse'. *October* 110: 2004.

David Graeber. *Possibilities: On Hierarchy, Rebellion, Desire*. Oakland: AK Press, 2007.

Carlo Ginzburg. *Threads and Traces: True, False, Fictive*. Berkeley: University of California Press, 2012.

*Carlo Ginzburg. *Clues, Myths, and the Historical Method*. Baltimore: Johns Hopkins University Press, 1989.

Bruno Gulli. *Labor of Fire: The Ontology of Labor Between Economy and Culture*. Temple University Press, 2005.

*Bruno Latour and Peter Weibel. *Making Things Public: Atmospheres of Democracy*. Cambridge, MA: MIT Press, 2005.

Paul Mason. *Postcapitalism*. London: Allen Lane, 2015.

Alessandro Portelli. *The Death of Luigi Trastulli and Other Stories*. Albany: State University of New York Press, 1991.

*Alessandro Portelli. *The Battle of Valle Giulia: Oral History and the Art of Dialogue*. Madison: University of Wisconsin Press, 1997.

Alessandro Portelli. *They Say in Harlan County: An Oral History*. New York: Oxford University Press, 2011.

Denise Riley. *The Words of Selves: Identification, Solidarity, Irony*. Stanford, CA: Stanford University Press, 2000.

Sally Sales. *Adoption, Family and the Paradox of Origins: A Foucauldian History*. Basingstoke: Palgrave Macmillan, 2012.

Marilyn Strathern. *Commons and Borderlands: Working Papers on Interdisciplinarity, Accountability and the Flow of Knowledge*. Wantage: Sean Kingston Publishing, 2004.

*Studs Terkel. *Hope Dies Last: Making a Difference in an Indifferent World*. London: Granta, 2005.

Studs Terkel. *The Good War*. Harmondsworth: Penguin, 1986.

Roberto Unger. *The Left Alternative*. London: Verso, 2009.

Raoul Vaneigem. *The Revolution of Everyday Life*. Trans. Donald Nicholson-Smith. Oakland: PM Press, 2012.

C. Wright Mills. *The Sociological Imagination*. New York: Oxford University Press, 1999.

About the Author

After dropping out of Cambridge University and running away to sea, Phil Cohen played a key role in London's counter culture scene of 1965–78. As "Dr John" he was the public face of the London street commune movement and the occupation of 144 Piccadilly, an event that briefly hit the world's headlines in July 1969. He subsequently became an urban ethnographer and gained an international reputation for his research on issues of race, class and youth culture. For the past forty years he has been involved with working-class communities in East London documenting the impact of structural and demographic change on their livelihoods, lifestyles, and life stories, culminating in two books on the impacts of the 2012 Olympics: *From the Wrong Side of the Track? East London and the Post Olympics* (2013) and the edited collection *London 2012 and the Post Olympics City: A Hollow Legacy?* (2017).

Currently he is research director of Livingmaps, a network of activists, artists, and academics developing a creative and critical approach to social mapping. He is also a professor emeritus at the University of East London and a senior research fellow of the Institute of Advanced Studies, University College London.

In addition to his academic writing, Cohen is the author of *Reading Room Only: Memoir of a Radical Bibliophile* (2013) and a collection of poetry and fiction, *Graphologies* (2014).

Index

"Passim" (literally "scattered") indicates intermittent discussion of a topic over a cluster of pages.

academic archives, 57, 58, 61
acquisition, 59, 60, 66, 67, 73, 92
'active mourning', 25, 111n33
actor-network theory (ANT), 91
adoption fantasies, 113n56
adoption history and archives, 38–39,
  80–82, 102–3, 107n3
Adorno, Theodor, 2, 6, 46
Agee, James: *Let Us Now Praise
  Famous Men*, 55–56
Albery, Nick, 109n18
Alexievich, Svetlana, 56; *Secondhand
  Time*, 36
alternative press, 18, 72, 77, 115n78.
  See also zines
alt-right, 53, 104–6
anamnesis and hypomnesis, 110n31
amnesia, social/cultural, xv, 48, 86, 88
anarchists and anarchism, 75, 76, 77,
  116n89
'anarchive', 93–97, 105, 106
'angel of history' (Benjamin), 42
Appadurai, Arjun, 68–69, 108n8
'archaeological fantasy', 101
'archive' (word), 1, 5–6
Archives of the Planet (Kahn), 91–92

archives, destruction of. *See*
  destruction of archives
archive types, 56–62
L'Archiviste (Schuiten and Peeters),
  51, 52
Ark of the Apostles Society, 5
art and artists, 88–90, 94–95, 97–100
audiovisual archives, 30

Bailey, Ron, 14
Bakhtin, Mikhail, 37, 116n84
Basile, Jonathan, 115n72
Beefsteak Club, 16
Benjamin, Walter, 6–7, 42, 55, 76, 95,
  98
Berlin Wall, 7–9
Bernstein, Basil: *Class, Codes and
  Control*, 116n83
bibliocide. *See* 'tomecide'
Bibliothèque Nationale, Paris, 119n121
BIT, 13, 109n18
Black Cultural Archive (BCA),
  Brixton, London, 63–71, 92
Bloch, Ernest, 41, 55
Boltanski, Christian, 97–98
'bonding' and 'bridging', 59–65
  passim, 77, 79, 91, 93, 105

books, digitalisation of, 48–49
Borges, Jorge Luis, 48, 49, 115n72
Bourdieu, Pierre, 115n82, 117n97
Bowie, David, 114n70
brain science. *See* cognitive science
Brexit, 104–5
'bridging' and 'bonding'. *See* 'bonding'
    and 'bridging'
British Library, 110n21
Brixton, London, 63–71
browsing, 49, 71, 74
buildings, 50, 64–65, 67–68, 119n121
buildings, squatting of. *See* squatters
    and squatting
burning or burying of personal
    effects, 25
Butler, Judith, 111n33

Cambridge University. *See* University
    of Cambridge
Castro, Fidel, 35
catalogues and cataloguing, 74, 76.
    See also classification
celebrity, 43, 46, 47, 53, 54, 59
censorship, 9, 81
charismatic authority, 44–45
Charlottesville, Virginia, 53
Children of Dijon (Boltanski), 97–98
'chrono-topography' (Bakhtin), 37, 40,
    113n58
Class, Codes and Control (Bernstein),
    116n83
class conflict, 100
classification, 60, 66, 76, 79, 92
class wars, 24, 87, 100
Clinton, Hillary, 107n3
closed archives, 39. *See also* 'dark
    archives'
cognitive science, 49
Cohen, Phil, xii–xv, 18–20; *Multi-
    racist Britain*, 97; *Reading Room
    Only*, 13
Common House, 75
Communist parties, 34–35, 43, 100,
    118n119
conceptual art, 88–90, 94–95

conjunctural archives, 57, 58, 68
conservation of archival materials,
    73, 93
consumerism, xiv, 11, 37, 47, 108n13
copyright law, 47
cult of personality. *See* personality
    cults
cultural capital, 38, 40, 96, 115n82,
    116n83
culture wars, 24, 87
curating, 62, 93–97, 101

'dark archives', 30, 43, 48, 57–58, 93,
    115n71
'dark tourism', 29, 90
death, 6, 23–27 passim, 43, 78, 90. *See
    also* immortality; legacy archives
    and legacy politics; mourning
Debord, Guy, 109n21
Demuth, Helene, 119n124
Derrida, Jacques, 3, 57, 110n31, 116n84
destruction of archives, 51, 88
détournement, 39, 109n21
digital archives, 7, 9, 48–50, 95–96,
    110n31, 115n71
digital culture, 7, 49, 95, 96, 108n8. *See
    also* social media
digitalisation, 73. *See also* books,
    digitalisation of; digital archives
'*dingpolitik*', 79, 82, 99, 101
D-I-Y Space, London, 75
do-it-yourself archives, 47, 50, 62, 96
donations and gifts of archival
    material, 66, 78, 92
Durant, Sam, 94

East Germany, 7–9
*Eighteenth Brumaire of Louis
    Napoleon* (Marx), 35
Engels, Friedrich, 55, 119n124
Ernst, Wolfgang, 2, 7
Escher, Wolfgang, 7
Evans, Walker: *Let Us Now Praise
    Famous Men*, 55–56

fabula and *syuzhet*, 60–65 passim, 116n84
'fake news', 20, 43, 105
false memory, 43, 106, 116n85
falsification, 8, 35. *See also* 'fake news'
fame, 46–48, 51, 53, 54
Farge, Arlette, 7, 101
feudalism, 33
First World War, 86
forgetting, 85–88 passim. *See also* amnesia, social/cultural
Foster, Hal, 94
Foucault, Michel, 3, 57, 90, 95
Freedom, 72, 116n89
Freud, Sigmund, 111n33, 112n43, 113n56, 116n85
Fuller, Samuel: *144 Piccadilly*, 14–15

Garrison, Len, 63, 64, 68
generations, xiii, 28, 29, 69
genocide, 29, 30, 31, 97
gentrification, 65, 71, 74, 76, 77, 92
German Ideology (Marx), 28
Germany, 88–90
Gerz, Jochen, and Esther Shalev-Gerz: Monument against Fascism, 88–90
Graeber, David, 83
Gramsci, Antonio, 2, 6, 7, 22, 31, 95, 98, 100
Greater London Council archives, 87, 110n26

hagiographic archives, 24, 57, 58, 68
Halbwachs, Maurice, 110n31
halls of fame, 46, 51, 54, 55
Hamburg, 88–90
heritage archives, 57, 58, 61, 65, 68
Heritage Lottery Fund, 65
Hermitage Museum, 36
heroes, 45, 55. *See also* hagiographic archives
The Hidden Injuries of Class (Sennett), 117
historiography, 'roots radical'. *See* 'roots radical' historiography
'history from below', 31

Holocaust, Jewish. *See* Jewish Holocaust
homeless people, 17–18, 110n25
Hopkins, John, 109n18
human progress. *See* progress
hypomnesis. *See* anamnesis and hypomnesis

iconic figures, 62. *See also* halls of fame; heroes
iconoclasm, 53
immortality, 32, 43–46 passim, 53–56
individuality, 20, 45, 80, 82
information overload, 48
Infoshop 56a, 69–77, 93
inheritance, history as, 27
'In Praise of Forgetting' (Rieff), 86–87
installations (art), 97–100
institutional archives, 57, 58
intellectual commons, 92, 96
intellectual property rights, 47, 96
Interference Archive, New York City, 93
internet, 73, 91. *See also* virtual archives
Istanbul, 41–42
Italy, 100

Jewish Holocaust, 30–31, 97
Judenplatz Holocaust Memorial, Vienna, 30–31

Kabakov, Ilya and Emilia, 98–100
Kahn, Albert, 91–92
Kings College Archive Centre, Cambridge, England, 5
kitsch, 41
Klein, Melanie, 111n33
Klein, Naomi: *No Logo*, 109n21

labour history, 59–60, 88. *See also* UK miners' strike of 1984
Labour Party (UK), 74, 77, 87, 88
Labyrinth (Kabakov), 99–100
Latour, Bruno, 3, 6, 91, 114n58
Lawrence, Stephen, 83, 111n34

Lee, Robert E., 53
'Left Archive', 82–85
'Left Field' (term), 84–85
legacy archives and legacy politics,
    22–31, 43–46, 61, 102–4
Lenin, Vladimir, 43, 55
Let Us Now Praise Famous Men (Agee
    and Evans), 55–56
librarianship, 94
libraries, 48–49, 110n21, 119n121. *See
    also* Infoshop 56a
'Library of Babel' (Borges), 48, 49,
    115n72
'Living Archive', 79–85 passim, 90–104
    passim
Livingmaps Network, 117n103
London, 87–88, 111n34; archives,
    63–78, 93, 110n26; Covent Garden,
    33, 113n49; mapping, 117n103;
    museums, 93; 1960s underground
    scene, xiv, 16–21 passim, 108n15,
    109n18; Subculture Archives,
    108n13
London Street Commune, 16, 17, 18
losers and winners. *See* winners and
    losers

Macuga, Goshka, 103
*The Man Who Flew into Space from
    His Apartment* (Kabakov), 99
maps and mapping, 70–71, 117n103
martyrology, 25–27
Marx, Karl, 55, 80, 82, 114n70;
    *Eighteenth Brumaire of Louis
    Napoleon*, 35; *German Ideology*, 28;
    The Poverty of Philosophy, 33–34;
    tomb, 103, 104
Marxists and Marxism, 34–35, 100,
    114n58
MayDay Rooms (MDR), xiv, 13, 16, 77,
    117n103
May 1968 fiftieth anniversary, 21
meeting spaces, 75
memory, 5, 24, 56–60 passim, 81, 86,
    97, 105; anamnesis and hypomnesis,
    110n31; in Boltanski installation, 98;
    collective/cultural, 7, 32, 43, 50, 51,
    64, 85, 91–95 passim; digital culture
    and, 49; narrative and, 49–50;
    short-term, 88. *See also* amnesia,
    social/cultural; false memory;
    forgetting; legacy archives and
    legacy politics; memoryscapes;
    mnemonic devices
memory boxes, 102–4
memoryscapes, 57, 68, 78, 86, 95, 100,
    102, 106
memory wars, 62
MetaArchive Cooperative, 48, 115n71
miners' strike of 1984. *See* UK miners'
    strike of 1984
mnemonic devices, 7, 24, 37, 90, 97,
    110n31; statues as, 53
modernity, 113–14n58. *See also* proto-
    modernism; retro-modernism
Modiano, Patrick, 2, 4
Momentum, 74, 77
Monument against Fascism (Gerz
    and Shalev-Gerz), 88–90
monuments and statues, 51, 53, 54, 87,
    88–90
mourning, 25, 27, 30, 85, 90, 103,
    111nn32–33
Multi-racist Britain (Cohen and Bains),
    67
museology, 59, 94, 101
Museum of Innocence, 41–42
museums, 16, 56, 87; dark archives,
    57–58; East Berlin, 7–8; Istanbul,
    41–42; London, 16, 93; Saint
    Petersburg, 36; Vienna, 30

narcissism, 11, 20, 46–47
narrative, 79, 82; in art assemblages,
    94–95; memory and, 49–50, 60–62
    passim
No Logo (Klein), 109n21
Nora, Pierre, 2, 5, 110n31
nostalgia, 4, 27, 41

obituaries, 44, 54
objects, meaning of, 78

occupation of 144 Piccadilly Street, London, 1969, 13–21

144 Piccadilly (Fuller), 14–15

open archives and 'open-source archives', 5, 94, 96, 107n3

open shelves, 71. *See also* browsing

optimism, 37; defeatism and, 31–32; of the will, 22, 38

oral history, 36, 51, 56, 100, 112n46

oral tradition, 25, 50

Orwell, George, 110n29

Pamuk, Orhan, 41–42

pantheon. *See* halls of fame

Peasants' Revolt (1381), 33

Peeters, Benoît: *L'Archiviste*, 51, 52

'The People United Will Never Be Defeated' (Rzewski), 32

personal effects, 25, 78

personality cults, 24, 45, 55

Personal Knowledge: Towards a Post-Critical Philosophy (Polanyi), 115–16n83

phantasy, 39; 113n56

photographs, 18–20, 27, 55, 91–92, 95, 115n71

physical location, 76. *See also* buildings

Piccadilly Street squat. *See* occupation of 144 Piccadilly Street, London, 1969

Polanyi, Michael: *Personal Knowledge*, 115–16n83

populist archives, 61, 81, 105–6

Portelli, Alessandro, 100

possessions, personal. *See* personal effects

postmodernism, 37, 113–14n58

poverty, 34, 55

The Poverty of Philosophy (Marx), 33–34

prefigurative politics, 83

preservation of archival materials. *See* conservation of archival materials

Presley, Elvis, 47

progress, 27, 37, 40

propaganda, 8, 9

proto-modernism, 37–45 passim, 58, 59, 78, 79, 113n58

Proudhon, Pierre-Joseph, 33

pseudo-archives, 43

reading, 49, 50

Reading Room Only (Cohen), 13

reading rooms, 67

realpolitik, 78, 82

Release, 13, 109n18

reputational identity, 23–24, 45, 51, 54, 57, 62

researchers' use of archives, 74

Resnais, Alain: *Toute la Mémoire du Monde*, 119n121

retro-modernism, 40–45 passim, 58, 59, 78, 105, 113n58

revisionism, 79, 86

Revolutionary Socialist Students Federation (RSSF), 14

Rhodes, Cecil, 53, 54

Rieff, David: 'In Praise of Forgetting', 86–87

'roots radical' historiography, 94, 118n107

Rubber Duck, 18

rubber stamps, 17

Ruskin College, Oxford, England, 88, 112n46

Russian Ark (Sokurov), 35–36

Russian art, 98–99

Rzewski, Frederic: 'The People United Will Never Be Defeated', 32

Saint Petersburg, 36

Samuels, Raphael, 112n46

Schuiten, François, *L'Archiviste*, 51, 52

Schumpeter, Joseph, 34

Science Museum, London, 93

Secondhand Time (Alexievich), 36

Second World War, 100

secret societies, 5

self-promotion, 43–44

Sennett, Richard: *The Hidden Injuries of Class*, 117n97
serendipity in research, 49
Shalev-Gerz, Esther. *See* Gerz, Jochen, and Esther Shalev-Gerz
Situationists, 14, 72, 109n21
social capital, 105, 115n82
social media, xv, 20, 46, 95–96
Sokurov, Alexandr: *Russian Ark*, 35–36
Soviet Union, 36, 43, 98–100
space, 73–74. *See also* buildings
squatters and squatting, xv, 13–21 passim, 71, 72, 74, 75
Stalin, Joseph, 43, 55
Stasi archives, 8
statues and monuments. *See* monuments and statues
Stiegler, Bernard, 110n31
Street Aid, 18, 110n25
street commune movement, 13–21
strikes, 22–23, 60, 87
Subculture Archives, London, 108
symbolic violence, 87, 117n97
syuzhet and *fabula*. See *fabula* and *syuzhet*

Terkel, Studs, 100
Thompson, E.P., 31
'tomecide', 48, 95
Toute la Mémoire du Monde (Resnais), 119n121
Trump, Donald, 53, 104–5

UK miners' strike of 1984, 22–23, 60, 87
underground press, 13, 18
Unger, Roberto, 90–91
United States, 53, 93, 104–5
University of Cambridge, 5
USSR. *See* Soviet Union

Vaneigem, Raoul, 90–91
Vasudevan, Alex, 74
Vienna, 30–31
virtual archives. *See* digital archives

war commemoration, 85–87
Warhol, Andy, 46
Weber, Max, 44
We Have Never Been Modern (Latour), 114n58
'what if' archives, 105
Whiteread, Rachel: Judenplatz Holocaust Memorial, 30–31
winners and losers, 31–37 passim, 69, 87
Witenagemot, 5–6
World War I. *See* First World War
World War II. *See* Second World War

zines, 72, 74
Žižek, Slavoj, 109n21

ABOUT PM PRESS

PM Press was founded at the end of 2007 by a small
collection of folks with decades of publishing, media, and
organizing experience. PM Press co-conspirators have
published and distributed hundreds of books, pamphlets,
CDs, and DVDs. Members of PM have founded enduring
book fairs, spearheaded victorious tenant organizing campaigns, and worked
closely with bookstores, academic conferences, and even rock bands to deliver
political and challenging ideas to all walks of life. We're old enough to know what
we're doing and young enough to know what's at stake.

We seek to create radical and stimulating fiction and non-fiction books, pamphlets,
T-shirts, visual and audio materials to entertain, educate, and inspire you. We
aim to distribute these through every available channel with every available
technology—whether that means you are seeing anarchist classics at our bookfair
stalls, reading our latest vegan cookbook at the café, downloading geeky fiction
e-books, or digging new music and timely videos from our website.

PM Press is always on the lookout for talented and skilled volunteers, artists,
activists, and writers to work with. If you have a great idea for a project or can
contribute in some way, please get in touch.

PM Press
PO Box 23912
Oakland, CA 94623
www.pmpress.org

FRIENDS OF PM PRESS

These are indisputably momentous times—the financial system is melting down globally and the Empire is stumbling. Now more than ever there is a vital need for radical ideas.

In the years since its founding—and on a mere shoestring— PM Press has risen to the formidable challenge of publishing and distributing knowledge and entertainment for the struggles ahead. With over 300 releases to date, we have published an impressive and stimulating array of literature, art, music, politics, and culture. Using every available medium, we've succeeded in connecting those hungry for ideas and information to those putting them into practice.

Friends of PM allows you to directly help impact, amplify, and revitalize the discourse and actions of radical writers, filmmakers, and artists. It provides us with a stable foundation from which we can build upon our early successes and provides a much-needed subsidy for the materials that can't necessarily pay their own way. You can help make that happen—and receive every new title automatically delivered to your door once a month—by joining as a Friend of PM Press. And, we'll throw in a free T-shirt when you sign up.

Here are your options:

- **$30 a month** Get all books and pamphlets plus 50% discount on all webstore purchases

- **$40 a month** Get all PM Press releases (including CDs and DVDs) plus 50% discount on all webstore purchases

- **$100 a month** Superstar—Everything plus PM merchandise, free downloads, and 50% discount on all webstore purchases

For those who can't afford $30 or more a month, we have **Sustainer Rates** at $15, $10 and $5. Sustainers get a free PM Press T-shirt and a 50% discount on all purchases from our website.

Your Visa or Mastercard will be billed once a month, until you tell us to stop. Or until our efforts succeed in bringing the revolution around. Or the financial meltdown of Capital makes plastic redundant. Whichever comes first.

Practical Utopia: Strategies for a Desirable Society

Michael Albert with a preface by Noam Chomsky

ISBN: 978-1-62963-381-7
$20.00   288 pages

Michael Albert's latest work, *Practical Utopia* is a succinct and thoughtful discussion of ambitious goals and practical principles for creating a desirable society. It presents concepts and their connections to current society; visions of what can be in a preferred, participatory future; and an examination of the ends and means required for developing a just society. Neither shying away from the complexity of human issues, nor reeking of dogmatism, *Practical Utopia* presupposes only concern for humanity.

Part one offers conceptual tools for understanding society and history, for discerning the nature of the oppressions people suffer and the potentials they harbor. Part two promotes a vision for a better way of organizing economy, polity, kinship, culture, ecology, and international relations. It is not a blueprint, of course, but does address the key institutions needed if people are to be free to determine their own circumstances. Part three investigates the means of seeking change using a variety of tactics and programs.

"*Practical Utopia immediately struck me because it is written by a leftist who is interested in the people winning and defeating oppression. The book is an excellent jumping off point for debates on the framework to look at actually existing capitalism, strategy for change, and what we need to do about moving forward. It speaks to many of the questions faced by grassroots activists who want to get beyond demanding change but who, instead, want to create a dynamic movement that can bring a just world into existence. As someone who comes out of a different part of the Left than does Michael Albert, I was nevertheless excited by the challenges he threw in front of the readers of this book. Many a discussion will be sparked by the arguments of this work.*"
—Bill Fletcher Jr., author of *"They're Bankrupting Us!" And 20 Other Myths about Unions*

"*Albert mulls over the better society that we may create after capitalism, provoking much thought and offering a generous, hopeful vision of the future. Albert's prescriptions for action in the present are modest and wise, his suggestions for building the future are ambitious and humane.*"
—Milan Rai

Anthropocene or Capitalocene? Nature, History, and the Crisis of Capitalism

Edited by Jason W. Moore

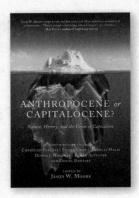

ISBN: 978-1-62963-148-6
$21.95   304 pages

The Earth has reached a tipping point. Runaway climate change, the sixth great extinction of planetary life, the acidification of the oceans—all point toward an era of unprecedented turbulence in humanity's relationship within the web of life. But just what is that relationship, and how do we make sense of this extraordinary transition?

Anthropocene or Capitalocene? offers answers to these questions from a dynamic group of leading critical scholars. They challenge the theory and history offered by the most significant environmental concept of our times: the Anthropocene. But are we living in the Anthropocene, literally the "Age of Man"? Is a different response more compelling, and better suited to the strange—and often terrifying—times in which we live? The contributors to this book diagnose the problems of Anthropocene thinking and propose an alternative: the global crises of the twenty-first century are rooted in the Capitalocene; not the Age of Man but the Age of Capital.

Anthropocene or Capitalocene? offers a series of provocative essays on nature and power, humanity, and capitalism. Including both well-established voices and younger scholars, the book challenges the conventional practice of dividing historical change and contemporary reality into "Nature" and "Society," demonstrating the possibilities offered by a more nuanced and connective view of human environment-making, joined at every step with and within the biosphere. In distinct registers, the authors frame their discussions within a politics of hope that signal the possibilities for transcending capitalism, broadly understood as a "world-ecology" that joins nature, capital, and power as a historically evolving whole.

Contributors include Jason W. Moore, Eileen Crist, Donna J. Haraway, Justin McBrien, Elmar Altvater, Daniel Hartley, and Christian Parenti.

"We had best start thinking in revolutionary terms about the forces turning the world upside down if we are to put brakes on the madness. A good place to begin is this book, whose remarkable authors bring together history and theory, politics and ecology, economy and culture, to force a deep look at the origins of global transformation."
—Richard Walker, professor emeritus of geography, UC Berkeley, and author of *The Capitalist Imperative, The New Social Economy, The Conquest of Bread,* and *The Country in the City*

In, Against, and Beyond Capitalism: The San Francisco Lectures

John Holloway
with a Preface by Andrej Grubačić

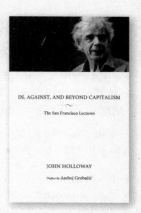

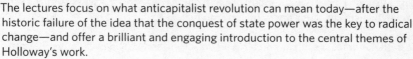

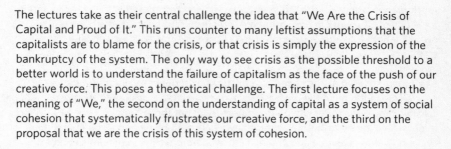

ISBN: 978-1-62963-109-7
$14.95   112 pages

In, Against, and Beyond Capitalism is based on three recent lectures delivered by John Holloway at the California Institute of Integral Studies in San Francisco. The lectures focus on what anticapitalist revolution can mean today—after the historic failure of the idea that the conquest of state power was the key to radical change—and offer a brilliant and engaging introduction to the central themes of Holloway's work.

The lectures take as their central challenge the idea that "We Are the Crisis of Capital and Proud of It." This runs counter to many leftist assumptions that the capitalists are to blame for the crisis, or that crisis is simply the expression of the bankruptcy of the system. The only way to see crisis as the possible threshold to a better world is to understand the failure of capitalism as the face of the push of our creative force. This poses a theoretical challenge. The first lecture focuses on the meaning of "We," the second on the understanding of capital as a system of social cohesion that systematically frustrates our creative force, and the third on the proposal that we are the crisis of this system of cohesion.

"His Marxism is premised on another form of logic, one that affirms movement, instability, and struggle. This is a movement of thought that affirms the richness of life, particularity (non-identity) and 'walking in the opposite direction'; walking, that is, away from exploitation, domination, and classification. Without contradictory thinking in, against, and beyond the capitalist society, capital once again becomes a reified object, a thing, and not a social relation that signifies transformation of a useful and creative activity (doing) into (abstract) labor. Only open dialectics, a right kind of thinking for the wrong kind of world, non-unitary thinking without guarantees, is able to assist us in our contradictory struggle for a world free of contradiction."
—Andrej Grubačić, from his Preface

"Holloway's work is infectiously optimistic."
—Steven Poole, the *Guardian* (UK)

"Holloway's thesis is indeed important and worthy of notice"
—Richard J.F. Day, *Canadian Journal of Cultural Studies*

Birth Work as Care Work: Stories from Activist Birth Communities

Alana Apfel, with a foreword by Loretta J. Ross, preface by Victoria Law, and introduction by Silvia Federici

ISBN: 978-1-62963-151-6
$14.95   128 pages

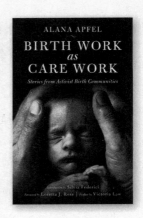

Birth Work as Care Work presents a vibrant collection of stories and insights from the front lines of birth activist communities. The personal has once more become political, and birth workers, supporters, and doulas now find themselves at the fore of collective struggles for freedom and dignity.

The author, herself a scholar and birth justice organiser, provides a unique platform to explore the political dynamics of birth work; drawing connections between birth, reproductive labor, and the struggles of caregiving communities today. Articulating a politics of care work in and through the reproductive process, the book brings diverse voices into conversation to explore multiple possibilities and avenues for change.

At a moment when agency over our childbirth experiences is increasingly centralized in the hands of professional elites, *Birth Work as Care Work* presents creative new ways to reimagine the trajectory of our reproductive processes. Most importantly, the contributors present new ways of thinking about the entire life cycle, providing a unique and creative entry point into the essence of all human struggle—the struggle over the reproduction of life itself.

"*I love this book, all of it. The polished essays and the interviews with birth workers dare to take on the deepest questions of human existence.*"
—Carol Downer, cofounder of the Feminist Women's Heath Centers of California and author of *A Woman's Book of Choices*

"*This volume provides theoretically rich, practical tools for birth and other care workers to collectively and effectively fight capitalism and the many intersecting processes of oppression that accompany it.* Birth Work as Care Work *forcefully and joyfully reminds us that the personal is political, a lesson we need now more than ever.*"
—Adrienne Pine, author of *Working Hard, Drinking Hard: On Violence and Survival in Honduras*

West of Eden: Communes and Utopia in Northern California

Edited by Iain Boal, Janferie Stone, Michael Watts, and Cal Winslow

ISBN: 978-1-60486-427-4
$24.95   304 pages

In the shadow of the Vietnam War, a significant part of an entire generation refused their assigned roles in the American century. Some took their revolutionary politics to the streets, others decided simply to turn away, seeking to build another world together, outside the state and the market. *West of Eden* charts the remarkable flowering of communalism in the '60s and '70s, fueled by a radical rejection of the Cold War corporate deal, utopian visions of a peaceful green planet, the new technologies of sound and light, and the ancient arts of ecstatic release. The book focuses on the San Francisco Bay Area and its hinterlands, which have long been creative spaces for social experiment. Haight-Ashbury's gift economy—its free clinic, concerts, and street theatre—and Berkeley's liberated zones—Sproul Plaza, Telegraph Avenue, and People's Park—were embedded in a wider network of producer and consumer co-ops, food conspiracies, and collective schemes.

Using memoir and flashbacks, oral history and archival sources, *West of Eden* explores the deep historical roots and the enduring, though often disavowed, legacies of the extraordinary pulse of radical energies that generated forms of collective life beyond the nuclear family and the world of private consumption, including the contradictions evident in such figures as the guru/predator or the hippie/entrepreneur. There are vivid portraits of life on the rural communes of Mendocino and Sonoma, and essays on the Black Panther communal households in Oakland, the latter-day Diggers of San Francisco, the Native American occupation of Alcatraz, the pioneers of live/work space for artists, and the Bucky dome as the iconic architectural form of the sixties.

Due to the prevailing amnesia—partly imposed by official narratives, partly self-imposed in the aftermath of defeat—*West of Eden* is not only a necessary act of reclamation, helping to record the unwritten stories of the motley generation of communards and antinomians now passing, but is also intended as an offering to the coming generation who will find here, in the rubble of the twentieth century, a past they can use—indeed one they will need—in the passage from the privations of commodity capitalism to an ample life in common.

"*As a gray army of undertakers gather in Sacramento to bury California's great dreams of equality and justice, this wonderful book, with its faith in the continuity of our state's radical-communitarian ethic, replants the seedbeds of defiant imagination and hopeful resistance.*"
—Mike Davis, author of *City of Quartz* and *Magical Urbanism*

Pictures of a Gone City: Tech and the Dark Side of Prosperity in the San Francisco Bay Area

Richard A. Walker

ISBN: 978-1-62963-510-1
$26.95   480 pages

The San Francisco Bay Area is currently the jewel in the crown of capitalism—the tech capital of the world and a gusher of wealth from the Silicon Gold Rush. It has been generating jobs, spawning new innovation, and spreading ideas that are changing lives everywhere. It boasts of being the Left Coast, the Greenest City, and the best place for workers in the USA. So what could be wrong? It may seem that the Bay Area has the best of it in Trump's America, but there is a dark side of success: overheated bubbles and spectacular crashes; exploding inequality and millions of underpaid workers; a boiling housing crisis, mass displacement, and severe environmental damage; a delusional tech elite and complicity with the worst in American politics.

This sweeping account of the Bay Area in the age of the tech boom covers many bases. It begins with the phenomenal concentration of IT in Greater Silicon Valley, the fabulous economic growth of the bay region and the unbelievable wealth piling up for the 1% and high incomes of Upper Classes—in contrast to the fate of the working class and people of color earning poverty wages and struggling to keep their heads above water. The middle chapters survey the urban scene, including the greatest housing bubble in the United States, a metropolis exploding in every direction, and a geography turned inside out. Lastly, it hits the environmental impact of the boom, the fantastical ideology of Tech World, and the political implications of the tech-led transformation of the bay region.

"San Francisco has battened from its birth on instant wealth, high-tech weaponry, and global commerce, and the present age is little different. Gold, silver, and sleek iPhones—they all glitter in the California sun and are at least as magnetic as the city's spectacular setting, benign climate, and laissez-faire lifestyles. The cast of characters changes, but the hustlers and thought-shapers eternally reign over the city and its hinterland, while in their wake they leave a ruined landscape of exorbitant housing, suburban sprawl, traffic paralysis, and delusional ideas about a market free enough to rob the majority of their freedom. Read all about it here, and weep."
—Gray Brechin, author of *Imperial San Francisco: Urban Power, Earthly Ruin*

"Walker has given us a brilliantly accessible and fact-laden political economy of the San Francisco Bay Area—America's richest and fastest changing metropolis. Pictures of a Gone City *explains both the miracle of Silicon Valley and the heavy price, in growing inequality, unaffordability, and environmental impact, that the Bay Area is paying for it."*
—Wendy Brown, author of *Undoing the Demos: Neoliberalism's Stealth Revolution*